PRIMERS

# Smart Cities

WILEY

PRIMERS

# Smart Cities

## A Spatialised Intelligence

# ANTOINE PICON

WILEY

A catalogue record for this book is available from the British Library.
ISBN 978-1-119-07559-2 (paperback) 978-1-119-07560-8 (ebk)
ISBN 978-1-119-07561-5 (ebk) 978-1-119-07562-2 (ebk)

Executive Commissioning Editor: Helen Castle
Project Editor: Miriam Murphy
Assistant Editor: Calver Lezama

Cover design, page design and layouts by Karen Willcox, www.karenwillcox.com
Printed in Italy by Printer Trento Srl
Cover image © Keiichi Matsuda

## Acknowledgements

In a book like this one, exchanges have a special importance. I would like to thank here the individuals involved in digital and smart city development, colleagues and friends, whose input has been very helpful to me. I am indebted to Joëlle Bitton, Jean Daniélou, François Ménard, Dominique Lorrain, François and Manuel Gruson, Nikola Jankovic, Nashid Nabian, Nicolas Nova, Colin O'Donnel, Carlo Ratti, Molly Wright Steenson and Ornella Zaza for their information and ideas. Special thanks to Marie Veltz who has shared with me the abundant documentation that she has gathered on smart cities.

My research has been facilitated by a Canadian Centre for Architecture Senior Mellon Fellowship. I would like to thank here Maristella Casciato, Mirko Zardini and Phyllis Lambert, who have been instrumental in making my stay at the Canadian Centre for Architecture especially fruitful.

Abigail Grater has done a wonderful job translating my sometimes intricate French into English. At Wiley, Helen Castle's constant support has proved invaluable. Caroline Ellerby has played an essential role in gathering the illustrations, a process that has proved quite challenging at times.

My deepest gratitude goes to Virginie Picon-Lefebvre whose careful reading and insightful comments have been, as always, essential.

# Contents

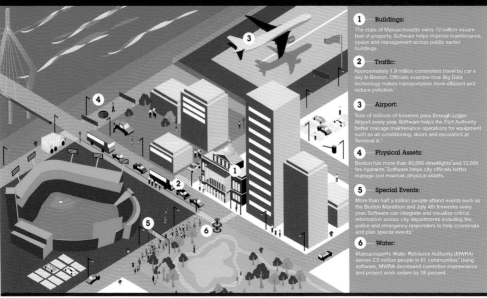

IBM, infographic on 'building a smarter city and state', 2013
IBM has played an important role in the rise of the smart city ideal. This infographic was released to illustrate a series of projects launched in partnership with the city of Boston and the state of Massachusetts. It features some key elements of the smart city approach such as a better management of urban infrastructure and the quest for greater environmental efficiency.

# Introduction
# A New
# Urban Ideal

Our cities are on the verge of a radical transformation, a revolution in intelligence comparable in scale to the one that, in its time, brought about industrialisation. The smart city, driven by digital technology, is poised to replace the typical networked city of the industrial era, whose success was built on its hard infrastructure, from roads to water supply and sanitation systems, not only as a technological optimum but also as a social and political project. This conviction is shared by many. Coined initially around 2005 to characterise a series of new urban uses of information and communications technology, the expression 'smart city' has spread everywhere, in both mass media and specialist literature, and in the discourse of businesses such as IBM and Cisco as well as out of the mouths of politicians. A new urban ideal is born; and this book is dedicated to it.

This ideal's increasing power has not prevented the existence of major ambiguities concerning the exact nature of the changes that are afoot. In the following pages, the different definitions of the smart city that are circulating today will be examined. It is worth noting immediately that they are almost all situated between two extremes: on one side, a limited meaning with an emphasis on optimisation of the city's functional aspects, and in particular of its infrastructure, through primarily digital tools; and on the other, a much broader vision that embraces not only the efficient management of facilities and services, but also the promotion of production and the exchange of knowledge – better quality of life through living more intelligently.

Beneath their apparent diversity, and despite the aforementioned opposition, the approaches to the smart city converge on several points. The first concerns the highly strategic character of information and communications technology, which is supposed to improve everyday city management at the same time as helping to make it more economical in terms of materials and energy – in a word, more ecological. On that subject, the need for sustainable development constitutes another point of convergence. Is it possible to speak of smart cities if urban zones continue, as they do today, to contribute to environmental degradation? There is likewise universal agreement on the importance of human factors. Whatever definition of the smart city one

**Aerial view of the Smart City Campus project, Barcelona, Spain, 2014**
The smart city ideal represents an important component of the urban strategy of Barcelona. It entails the revitalisation of a former industrial area through the creation of a campus bringing together businesses, universities and other players involved in urban technology and innovation.

prefers, the phenomenon calls for new types of both individual and collective behaviour. Without people who are capable of modelling their conduct on the information that they supply, the sensors, microchips and display screens of the smart city would have only a limited impact. Contrary to the arguments of its less informed detractors, the looming new urban revolution cannot be reduced, even in its narrowest sense, to a mere plan to equip the city with digital tools. It is inherently linked to questions of anthropology, sociology and, ultimately, politics.

As if echoing the opposition between the managerial vision and the broader interpretation of the notion of the smart city, two types of political projects are emerging today. The first focuses on controlling the urban organism, in an outlook not dissimilar to cybernetic research of the period from 1950 to 1970 into the running of complex systems. Such an orientation carries risks of technocratic drifting, and it is this that the other major project type which features in debate today – cities that call more upon the initiative of and cooperation between individuals than on co-ordination driven from above – seeks to prevent. Neocybernetic inspiration with technocratic overtones, or new perspectives of democratisation linked to the spread of information and communications technology? In the following chapters, this tension will be studied in more detail, and then overcome; because it is possible, under certain conditions that will be outlined, to envisage both of these orientations mutually supporting one another instead of being in conflict. When it has reached maturity, the smart city will be characterised by improved control of some of its key aspects, such as the functioning of its infrastructure, and by an increase in the creative potential of the human individuals and groups that inhabit it.

**Looking at smartphones, Kivus, Democratic Republic of Congo, 2012**
From highly industrialised to developing countries, smart cities are fundamentally about people. This explains the essential role played by mobile phones and particularly by smartphones in their rise.

## Spatialised Intelligence

Among the current proliferation of attempts at theorising, this book possesses two major points of originality. Firstly, it proposes taking the expression 'smart city' much more literally than is usually the case. Rather than conceiving of a city whose circuits of information and communications are simply sprawled out and whose intelligence continues to reside exclusively within the men and women who communicate through them, why not imagine the progressive development of non-human forms of reasoning and even of consciousness? At the final stage of such development, the seeds of which have already been sown in current research on algorithms, artificial intelligence, robotisation and cyborg-type assemblies between biological organisms and machines, the entire city could be considered intelligent in a new way, founded on the interaction and composition of the perceptions and deliberations of multiple entities: human, non-human and often a mixture of the two. At the heart of this greater, composite intelligence, which would at last make the famous 'general will' on which Jean-Jacques Rousseau based his *Of the Social Contract, or Principles of Political Right* (1762) more tangible, these entities would appear both as partially autonomous stakeholders and as subsystems constituting the city's general intelligence.[1]

Human and iCub robot, Institut des Systèmes Intelligents et de Robotique (ISIR), Université de Paris VI, 2013
The iCub has been designed to act like a baby. Its purpose is to explore how human cognition develops by learning in the same way a child would. The research is typical of the rapid progress being made in robotics and artificial intelligence.

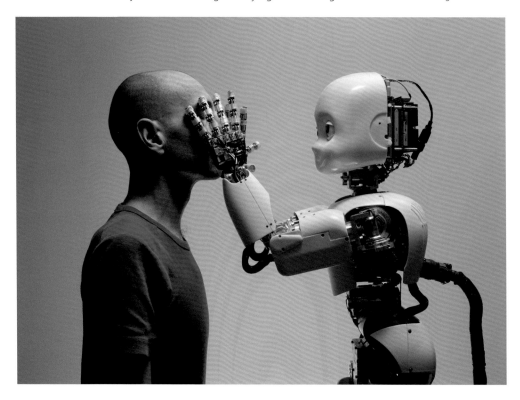

For those who prefer Leibniz to Rousseau, it is also possible to consider them as sorts of monads: specific viewpoints on a whole, the city, which contains them all and which each of them contains in its entirety.[2]

Is this all science fiction? Of course; but, without falling into the mystique of technological progress definitively replacing human intelligence with that of machines – the 'singularity' that is tirelessly proclaimed by Ray Kurzweil, one of the main prophets of the 'post-human' condition – it is hard not to be struck by the rapidly progressing capacities of perception and reasoning displayed by the machines and systems around us.[3] Is the smart city science fiction? Undoubtedly so; but, as we will see, the accounts that are written about it have a highly self-fulfilling character: that is, they generate the conditions that make them feasible, in the same way as some political or economic forecasts influence voting dynamics or market behaviour by causing them to lean in the direction that makes them possible.

This intelligence should not be considered as a capacity residing principally in central processing units and the memory of specialist servers, in the manner of the supercomputer HAL 9000 portrayed by Stanley Kubrick in *2001: A Space Odyssey* (1968). On the contrary, it should be envisaged as being distributed right across the city, present in the sensors and chips with which the infrastructure, streets and buildings are fitted, as well as in the numerous electronic devices belonging to its inhabitants. The smart city is a city activated at millions of points, thanks to information and communications technology. Since it is spread out, and since it follows the topography of the networks of streets and buildings as well as the movement of vehicles and of its inhabitants, producing a map of urban activity in real time, its intelligence is profoundly spatial.

The attention paid to this spatial dimension constitutes a second specificity of this book's approach. This may appear paradoxical, since the development of information technology has long been associated with a sort of annihilation of space. In the mid-19th century, when Samuel Morse developed his telegraph system, his contemporaries celebrated what they saw as the definitive victory of intelligence over distance.[4] The same refrain was later taken up in relation to the telephone, radio, television, and more recently the Internet.

But digital technologies, now in their maturity, have restored the importance of space. They often involve geolocation: that is, the ability to know the position of a multitude of stationary or moving objects, in real time.

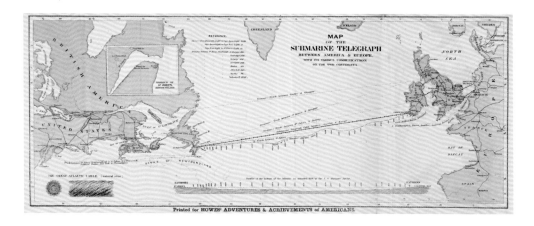

Printed for HOWES' ADVENTURES & ACHIEVEMENTS of AMERICANS.

They enhance physical reality by enriching three-dimensional space with contextual electronic content. Geolocation and augmented reality are two fundamental dimensions of a sort of return to space, or 'spatial turn', to use the expression coined by urban geographer Edward Soja in relation to the recent evolution of the social sciences.[5] This spatial turn of digital technologies has been reinforced by the multiplication of electronic interfaces and the proliferation of wireless communications, which make it possible to speak of ubiquitous or ambient computing. These evolutions constitute the foundations on which the smart city can begin to be built.

However – and this is a second paradox – they have not modified the physical structure of the city. Everything continues as if the city were progressively coming alive, but without bodily changes for the time being. It must obviously be assumed that such a process will soon be accompanied by morphological transformations. Several precursory signs support this hypothesis. One of this book's objectives is to raise awareness among urbanists and architects, and more generally anyone interested in the future of built-up areas, of the issues around these transformations which the spatial quality of city intelligence will render inevitable.

Although the form of cities has not yet evolved, urban mapping has undergone a series of rapid and spectacular shifts. As we will see, the spread of geographic information systems (GIS) is far from being the only manifestation of this phenomenon. Digital maps produced by collectives, such as OpenStreetMap or those used on mobile phones and tablets, may well be a prelude to a far more radical revolution in urban representation

Henry Howe, 'Map of the Submarine Telegraph between America & Europe', 1858
The collapse of space has been among the most enduring myths of the industrial age. In the mid-19th century, the telegraph was already supposed to have abolished distance. The same has been said of the Internet in its early stages of development. We are now beginning to realise that what is happening is rather a hybridisation between physical and electronic spaces.

and in the relationship between cities and citizens. In this respect, the map appears as one of the preferred ways to express the city's nascent intelligence. This is why it is explored at length in the present volume.

## Technology, Space and Politics

The book tackles these questions with an argument that ranges from examination of the transformations already experienced by many cities in the face of the progressive emergence of spatialised intelligence, to discussion of the social and political implications of this process. This social and political dimension is particularly important. Cities, more than nation-states, are a melting pot of new forms of sociability and collective action founded on an association between humans and non-humans.

The first chapter is dedicated to discussing the notion of the smart city and the self-fulfilling character of the many narratives relating to it. Behind these narratives are the most striking current achievements, such as infrastructure and flow management, which rely on the proliferation of sensors and chips that make it possible to track, often in real time, what is going on in the city. Through digital technology, urban space seems to be becoming receptive to the events and situations that affect it, in a similar way to how organisms become sensitised. This process recalls the story of the statue evoked by the French Enlightenment philosopher Étienne Bonnot de Condillac in his

Screenshot from 'Nokia City Lens', Nokia's augmented-reality application for its Lumia smartphones, 2013
The application uses the phone's viewfinder and Nokia's mapping platform to give information regarding the nearby shops, cafés and restaurants of interest. Smartphones have been instrumental in the development of augmented reality.

*Traité des sensations* [*Treatise on Sensations*] (1754). Initially deprived of the five senses, Condillac's statue successively acquires smell, hearing, taste, sight and finally touch, as it progressively gains awareness of the world around it and of its own self. Thanks to digital technology, the city seems to have embarked on a similar journey. The sensitised city is also one in which sensory satisfaction generates strategies intended to foster loyalty among an educated urban population which authors such as Richard Florida and Edward Glaeser place within the principle of the new 'knowledge economy' that is supposed to be replacing the old industrial economy – although this substitution has yet to be proved universal.[6]

Both sentient and sensual, the smart city is based on the identification of millions of elementary occurrences – from evaluating individuals' consumption of water and electricity, to recording motor traffic at specific hotspots on the road network, to measuring atmospheric pollution. These occurrences, which are often put together to generate more general statistics that can be brought up on computer screens in the form of maps or tables, reinforce the event-based character of a city that seems to be made up of everything that is going on within it. While the networked city inherited from the 19th century was almost exclusively based on flow management, the smart city promises to master events, situations and scenarios.

With this observation as a starting point, the book's second chapter shows how this reading of the city, in terms of occurrences and events that lead to situations and allow scenarios to be constructed, can feed into plans to control the urban organism through digital platforms, the development of which is mobilising companies such as Cisco, IBM and Siemens. Such projects seem to relate to the desire to pilot complex systems that drove cybernetics throughout the 1950s and 1960s. In the domain of the smart city, we are indeed witnessing the emergence of projects inspired by neocybernetics, based on an ideal of the hierarchical control of information and of the behaviour that results from it. In contrast to this interpretation of the new urban ideal, which can easily be criticised for its technocratic tendency, is a more participatory vision founded on individuals cooperating freely, following the example of businesses such as Wikipedia. Top-down city or bottom-up city? Neocybernetics-inspired city or collaborative city? The future intelligence of cities will reside in the coexistence of these two approaches, and above all in the interactions that such a cohabitation is sure to provoke. It may immediately be noted that a whole array of intermediaries exist between technocratically inspired control and freely consented cooperation. The social

Eric Fischer, map of New York with the location of pictures posted on Flickr by locals and tourists between 5 and 10 June 2010
Blue dots correspond to pictures taken by locals, red to pictures taken by tourists, yellow ones are by unspecified authors. Whereas their physical structure has not yet changed, cities are deeply transformed by the proliferation of online content that seems to endow them with a new form of life.

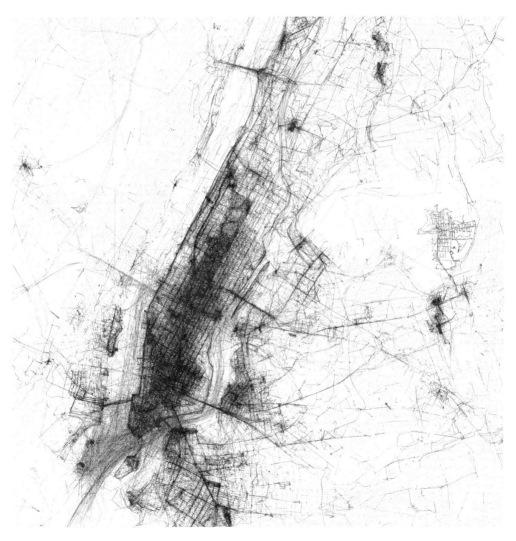

media, for example, headed by Facebook, following the very undemocratic definition of their general operating rules, have resorted to forms of control that rely on individuals and their capacity to self-regulate by coordinating among themselves through swarm behaviour.

Finally, the book's last chapter explores the spatialised character of city intelligence more deeply, starting with geolocation and augmented reality.

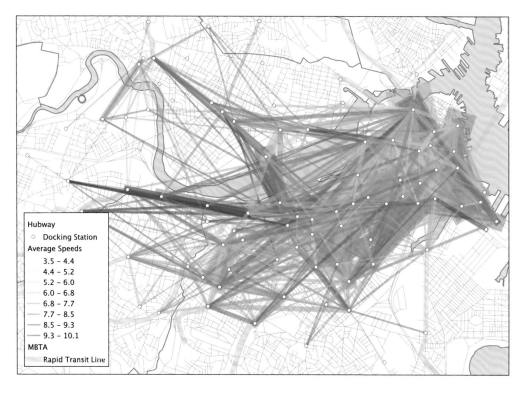

In total contrast to the seeming absence of any impact of digital technology on urban form, this spatialised character allows a better understanding of the crucial role played by mapping, a booming field that reflects the tension between control and cooperation. While it draws heavily on the resources offered by geolocation and augmented reality, the map constitutes one of the best ways to make information accessible, especially in the case of big data which is more and more often involved today. The SENSEable City Lab at the Massachusetts Institute of Technology (MIT) specialises in this cartographic treatment of massive quantities of data, such as those collected by mobile phone operators.[7] In many cases, mapping makes visible the dividing line between what is revealed to the public and what remains reserved for narrow circles of specialists and political leaders. At the same time, it contributes to the emergence of what the French philosopher Jacques Rancière calls 'the distribution of the sensible' – that is, 'the system of self-evident facts of sense perception that simultaneously discloses the existence of something in common and the delimitations that define

Ari Ofsevit, map showing the speeds between the docking stations of the bike-sharing system Hubway in Boston, Massachusetts, 2012
Mapping has become a key practice in order to visualise and understand the massive quantities of data produced by cities today. Maps suggest innovative ways to manage and use the various urban infrastructures, from energy grids to bike-sharing systems.

the respective parts and positions within it'.[8] Because the rise of digital technology and the advent of the smart city do not both come under the aegis of absolute visibility. Certain information is made accessible to all, while other data require a specific qualification and/or a particular position in the institutional hierarchy. By the same token, visibility has become a social and political problem. Founded on a dual process of the revelation, often through maps, and distribution of data that are too technical or sensitive to be shown to all and sundry, such as those involving pollution or crime, today's urban transformations give rise to numerous questions situated at the crossroads of aesthetics – in Rancière's sense as the active ingredient in 'the distribution of the sensible' – and politics.

This book is the last part of an investigation that has extended over more than 15 years on the links between the increasing power of computer and digital technology, spatial transformations, and cultural and political dynamics. Having begun at the urban scale with an essay on the 'city as cyborg territory', I continued my inquiry with a closer examination of recent architectural evolution, from the general conception of buildings to the return of ornamental practices that are marked by numerous issues, dedicating two books to this evolution: *Digital Culture in Architecture* and *Ornament: The Politics of Architecture and Subjectivity*.[9] There are many links between my reflections here on the smart city, and these earlier publications: for example, the particular attention paid to imagination and storytelling; the importance accorded to the development of an event-based approach to architecture and cities; and, most of all, the central role

**IBM Rio de Janeiro Operations Center, 2014**
This emblematic realisation of IBM for the city of Rio de Janeiro is permeated by a distinct neocybernetic inspiration. Its aim is to manage crucial aspects of urban life, including major events like the final match of the 2014 football World Cup, in real time.

played, in my opinion, by the emergence of new forms of subjectivity that are contemporary with the rise of the digital.

Throughout this investigation, and especially where smart cities were concerned, I aimed to avoid the twin pitfalls of unbridled enthusiasm for technology and blanket criticism – two attitudes which are unfortunately all too common in relation to digital matters. In the field of technology, change is never unequivocal, entirely positive or negative. It generally takes the form of a complex amalgam of both improvement and worsening of what already exists. Some things seem good, while others seem to herald a future of disillusionment; because technological change is inseparable from social and political issues. Technology changes in line with the evolution of society and its institutions. From this point of view, smart cities cannot provide a remedy for all the problems that besiege us. They signify a turning point, but one which – like those that came before it, such as urban change brought on by industrialisation in particular – will consist of both advantages and disadvantages. Some of these will be outlined at the end of the book.

The affirmation that technological change is unavoidably social and political should not lead to a confusion between technology and society. It is more worthwhile to credit technology with the capacity to influence the form of social, political and economic organisations, if not from the outside then at least with a scope that cannot be reduced merely to the forward march of capitalism. In this respect, the notion of the co-production of science, technology and society proposed by the American expert in science and

OpenStreetMap mapping party at the Stamen Design office in San Francisco, 26 April 2014
Collaborative enterprises like OpenStreetMap often organise 'parties' in which people are teamed up to gather and input data. A real party with food and drinks usually follows.

technology studies Sheila Jasanoff seems more interesting than the ritual reaffirmation of the primacy of social matters.[10]

Similarly, it would seem useful to resist the temptation of reducing space to a mere product of society, ignoring everything that it owes to a sort of intrinsic obstinacy of things, materials, objects and distances, as well as to the way in which the disciplines of planning, architecture, engineering and urbanism play on the constraints that it engenders. The spatialised intelligence of cities of the future will also carry the mark of this obstinacy and these plans. Here again, the notion of co-production proves useful. Neither blindly enthusiastic nor exaggeratedly critical, not seeking to be reassured by assimilating technology and social matters just like that or by interpreting space purely in the light of social relationships: these are the conditions under which it becomes possible to grasp the character, both exciting and worrying, of what is emerging before our very eyes – a new kind of city, together with political issues with no past equivalent.

# References

1 Jean-Jacques Rousseau, *Of the Social Contract, or Principles of Political Right* [*Du contrat social ou, Principes du droit politique*, 1762], English translation, Harper & Row (New York), 1984.
2 Gottfried Wilhelm Freiherr von Leibniz, *Discourse on Metaphysics; and, The Monadology* [*Discours de métaphysique*, 1686 and *La Monadologie*, 1714], English translation, Prometheus Books (Buffalo, New York), 1992.
3 Ray Kurzweil, *The Singularity is Near: When Humans Transcend Biology*, Penguin (New York), 2005.
4 Vincent Mosco, *The Digital Sublime: Myth, Power, and Cyberspace*, MIT Press (Cambridge, Massachusetts), 2004, p 119.
5 Edward W Soja, *Postmodern Geographies: The Reassertion of Space in Critical Social Theory*, Verso (London), 1989.
6 Richard Florida, *The Rise of the Creative Class: And How It's Transforming Work, Leisure, Community, and Everyday Life*, Basic Books (New York), 2002; Edward Glaeser, *Triumph of the City: How Our Greatest Invention Makes Us Richer, Smarter, Greener, Healthier, and Happier*, Penguin Press (New York), 2011.
7 See http://senseable.mit.edu/ (consulted 11 November 2014).
8 Jacques Rancière, *The Politics of Aesthetics* [*Le Partage du sensible: Esthétique et politique*, 2000], translated by Gabriel Rockhill, Continuum (London and New York), 2004, p 12.
9 Antoine Picon, *La Ville territoire des cyborgs*, Les Editions de l'Imprimeur (Besançon), 1998; Antoine Picon, *Digital Culture in Architecture: An Introduction for the Design Professions*, Birkhäuser (Basel), 2010; Antoine Picon, *Ornament: The Politics of Architecture and Subjectivity*, Wiley (Chichester), 2013.
10 On the notion of co-production, see for instance Sheila Jasanoff (ed), *States of Knowledge: The Co-Production of Science and the Social Order*, Routledge (New York), 2004.

# 1

# The Advent of the Smart City, from Flow Management to Event Control

What is it that makes a city 'smart'? While the expression 'smart city' is American in origin, the reflections and experimentation to which it refers are not the preserve of a single country or culture; far from it. They are emerging everywhere: in Korea as well as in the United States, and in France and Spain along with the United Kingdom and Scandinavia. Though it may spontaneously spark off thoughts of metropolises at the cutting edge of technology such as London, New York and Singapore, it also concerns many other towns. IBM's Smarter Cities Challenge, which aims to promote the technological solutions conceived by the company to improve urban administration and services, embraces around a hundred cities, including a number of medium-sized ones such as Faro in Portugal and Syracuse in Sicily. This IBM initiative ignores the dividing line between rich and developing countries. Consequently, Ahmedabad in India and Medellín in Colombia feature among the list of towns concerned by the Challenge.[1] An estimated total of nearly 39.5 billion American dollars of investment is due to be made in the field of smart cities in 2016, compared with a total of just 8.1 billion in 2010.[2]

## Defining the Smart City

The global success of the notion of smart cities is matched in scale by the ambiguities attached to it. And yet, the technical infrastructure that it involves and the general objectives that are assigned to it seem clear at first glance. The smart city relies on intensive use of information and communications technology. It works through the development of electronic content and the increasing hybridisation of the latter with the physical world, a mingling that is often described as 'augmented reality'. Its construction engages with a number of key issues, such as the possibility of reconciling the quality of urban life with sustainable development through close management of technological resources and infrastructure. A 2008 report estimated the reduction in carbon emissions that would be obtained by the development of information and communications technologies by 2020 at 15 per cent of the former year's figures.[3] In turn, a more recent study gauged this reduction, again by 2020, at more than 18 per cent of the 2011 total.[4] Besides smart grids and other highly reactive networks that should allow an optimisation of the urban metabolism, the smart city is meant to offer new opportunities to individuals equipped with mobile devices, and to allow new collectives to emerge, along the lines of organisations such as Wikipedia and OpenStreetMap that involve collaboration on a massive scale.

By this point, a string of ambiguities are already emerging. How far should the scope of the notion of the smart city extend? Should it encompass all the aspirations that are being expressed today, for a better quality of urban living based on the marriage of digital technology with the quest for sustainability and the sharing of experiences and knowledge? In considering this, two possible pitfalls need to be avoided. The first is in opting for an overly narrow definition of the smart city centred purely on the use of digital technology – an often covert technological determinism – in which we either attribute all sorts of socially beneficial effects to technology, or, on the contrary, hold it responsible for new pathologies, while at the same time denying that we want to reduce the range of possibilities to the consequences of technology alone. The other pitfall is in choosing instead an overly broad definition: one involving a dilution of the undeniable impact of a series of technological developments, including ubiquitous computing, geolocation and augmented reality, all of which will crop up frequently throughout this book.

But the main source of ambiguity, or even disagreement, in relation to smart cities stems from the type of stakeholder seen as responsible for sparking off a dynamic that appears more and more as a new urban ideal – an ideal that is even dressed up as utopian in the writings of certain authors whose technophilia knows no limits. In contrast to the latters' enthusiasm, the most critical commentators on this ideal often interpret it as the result of strategies formed by large corporate groups such as Cisco, IBM and Siemens, which redirected themselves towards urban issues under the influence of factors such as the 2008 financial crisis that lowered the value of many firms' investments in information and communications technology. The exponential market growth of the smart city justifies this choice a posteriori. This very corporate vision usually goes in tandem with a close focus on projects such as Songdo International Business District

**Living PlanIT, concept plan for PlanIT Valley, Portugal, 2010**
Located in the north of Portugal and conceived by the company Living PlanIT, the developer of an urban-oriented software platform, PlanIT Valley seeks to offer a model for the city of the future and serve as a laboratory for smart technologies.

in South Korea, Masdar City in Abu Dhabi and PlanIT Valley in northern Portugal: new urban developments from scratch, which act as showcases for the service platforms offered by the firms. This reduction of the smart city to these new cities that belong to a genre founded on a close association of physical and digital infrastructures goes hand in hand with the denunciation of attempts to reduce the city to a well-oiled mechanism, a new avatar of these brave new worlds that periodically give rhythm to the history of urbanism. In a stimulating pamphlet very pointedly entitled *Against the Smart City*, published in 2013, the American urbanist Adam Greenfield had no trouble contrasting the complexity of existing cities with the inadequacy of an approach that, in his view, adopted the functionalist credo of modern architecture and urbanism.[5] The American sociologist Richard Sennett told a fairly similar tale in an article that appeared the previous year in *The Guardian*, on the occasion of a conference organised in London on the theme of the smart city; again, he contrasted the mechanical character of Masdar and Songdo with the creative spontaneity of metropolises such as Chicago and Mumbai.[6] Although he does not limit the question of the smart city to new urban developments started from scratch, Rem Koolhaas has recently taken up the same sort of argument.[7]

**Living PlanIT, energy mix scheme for PlanIT Valley, Portugal, 2010**
Among the ambitions of the project is an energy scheme combining various sources: solar, wind and hydraulic, along with anaerobic digestion. Smart and sustainable are considered as almost synonymous.

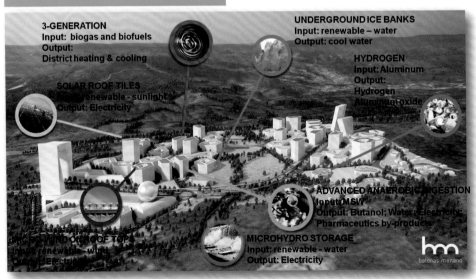

LIVING PLANIT - Energy Mix

**3-GENERATION**
Input: biogas and biofuels
Output:
District heating & cooling

**UNDERGROUND ICE BANKS**
Input: renewable – water
Output: cool water

**HYDROGEN**
Input: Aluminum
Output:
Hydrogen
Aluminum oxide

**SOLAR ROOF TILES**
Input: renewable - sunlight
Output: Electricity

**WIND ON ROOF TOPS**
Input: renewable - wind
Output: Electricity

**ADVANCED ANAEROBIC DIGESTION**
Input: MSW
Output: Butanol; Water; Electricity;
Pharmaceutics by-products

**MICROHYDRO STORAGE**
Input: renewable - water
Output: Electricity

balonas menano

Even if they are partly justifiable, these attacks reveal a certain type of amnesia with regard to the importance and inventiveness of initiatives set up by firms in the field of urban technology. For example, electricity arrived in American and European towns in the late 19th and early 20th centuries under the initiative of companies such as Edison, Westinghouse and Siemens, who understood the potential of the newly emerging market more quickly than others.[8]

The example of electricity is interesting for another reason also: because the dynamic of urban electrification cannot be reduced to these companies' strategies alone. Far from it; for it brings into play an infinitely broader ensemble of stakeholders, politicians, municipal employees and clients, each with their own expectations and behaviours. Concerning expectations, imagination also has its place in this process, as witness the extraordinary futuristic visions of the French illustrator Albert Robida from the late 19th and early 20th centuries. Electrification would therefore appear to be a complex dynamic that cannot be condensed purely into the logic of capitalist profit, even though the latter did drive the movement forward.

As a specialist in the application of digital technology to the urban scene, the American researcher Anthony Townsend shows a clear understanding of this irreducibility in his inspiring book on smart cities, even though he also acknowledges the pioneering role played by large information and communications technology firms worried by the fall in private investments in their sector after the 2008 crash.[9] Besides Cisco and IBM, he notably cites the role of another category of stakeholders whom he describes as 'civic hackers': software developers working independently or for city councils, who use the massive quantities of data that have been made available by digital technology to promote more collaborative urban practices. He points to the 'Foursquare' app – which allows its users to exchange information and opinions on cafés, restaurants and shops – as an alternative approach to the smart city based on individual and collective initiatives. In his book, Townsend also gives considerable attention to the sort of imagination which he sees as bordering on utopianism.

Besides civic hackers, many other stakeholders are also involved, starting with the users of digital technology who are being called upon to participate more and more actively in the smart city. The discussion around the smart city cannot be summarised simply by the choice between big business and civic hackers. This is why I have opted to contrast the neocybernetic approach with projects that are more participatory in inspiration, whether they be undertaken by municipal administrations (as in Paris), developers or groups of users.

Two other limitations of Townsend's book lie in his relative indifference to the concrete characteristics of urban space – the cities he discusses remain strangely insubstantial – and above all in a definition of city intelligence that remains fairly conventional, all things considered. Like most other commentators before him, Townsend struggles to imagine that the intelligence of cities could be beyond the grasp of the various brains that inhabit them. Of course, cities have always been intelligent in the sense that they efficiently bring together people who possess powers of reason. It would however seem that the increasing hybridisation of humankind and technology, which accompanies the rise of the digital, invites a more fundamental reconsideration of the question.

What is a smart city? This book adopts a hypothesis that is both simple and radical: where the intelligence of cities is concerned, the term 'intelligence' needs to be taken much more literally than may seem to be the case. Intelligence in the sense of the ability to learn, understand and reason. The underlying ambition of many current projects and experiments is to make existing cities intelligent, or even in some sense conscious. This ambition cannot be reduced to the scope of available technologies, as it goes far beyond what they prescribe. This certainly explains why Townsend pays it so little attention. By the same token, the smart city appears as the fruit of a dynamic that is only

**Cover of Albert Robida's** *Le Vingtième siècle: La Vie électrique*, **Librairie Illustrée (Paris), 1892** On the eve of the 20th century, the French illustrator Albert Robida depicted all sorts of spectacular applications of electricity to everyday life, sometimes visionary, sometimes imbued with irony.

Albert Robida, *Téléphonoscope*, from *Le Vingtième siècle: La Vie électrique*, 1892
More than a century before the development of massive open online courses (MOOCs), Robida imagined the development of networked distance learning through the use of the *téléphonoscope*, a machine conceived as an extension of the telephone in the domain of image transmission.

LES COURS PAR TÉLÉPHONOSCOPE.

partially technological. At the same time, the temptation of determinism, with its techno-optimist and techno-pessimist corollaries and their heady scents of utopia and anti-utopia, is foiled. The opposite risk of minimising the impact of technology is likewise set aside, since the essential novelty of the intelligence that is emerging before our very eyes stems from its partially non-human character and from an unprecedented association between humankind, machines and algorithms.

What is a smart city? Having outlined the various current stances on the subject, it appears to be both an ideal and a process. As an ideal, it consists of a city whose digital tools allow the optimisation of its functioning and sustainability, as well as of its inhabitants' quality of life and the types of relationships they can maintain with one another. In so doing, this city demonstrates a form of intelligence with no past equivalent. In the smart city, some mechanisms for learning, understanding and reasoning are internalised; they become intrinsic to the city itself, instead of residing in the minds of the humans who live in it.

Screenshot of the 'Foursquare' United States website, 2015
A local search and discovery service launched in 2008, Foursquare had some 45 million registered users by the end of 2013. Users can post reviews, recommendations and ratings of venues, thus promoting a more participative approach to the city.

This ideal presents contradictions which are not masked in this book. But they are softened by a development dynamic that declares them to have been overcome. Because the smart city also appears as a process. From this point of view, our cities are already intelligent, or at least rapidly becoming so, under the effect of a complex group of factors including, of course, the technological innovations, business strategies and civic hackers' projects so dear to Townsend, but also the actions of millions of anonymous stakeholders who are experimenting with a new relationship to the urban environment in which the human and the non-human are becoming more entangled by the day.

## Self-Fulfilling Fictions

While specialists in urban matters still have difficulty conceiving of the notion that cities might be able to access an autonomous form of intelligence, science fiction has less trouble making that leap. Indeed, intelligent cities, and even cities that possess a form of consciousness, have long haunted novelists' and filmmakers' imaginations. One of the most radical versions of the intelligent city features in the American author Joe Haldeman's novel *The Accidental Time Machine*, published in 2007.[10] The story involves an artificial intelligence called La that governs the city of Los Angeles. La – which is also of course the acronym of the Californian metropolis – can take on all sorts of forms, although she normally presents herself to her interlocutors as a woman. She can appear in an infinite number of places at once, especially when local taxes are due to be paid by the city's residents. During this tense period, she appears, in a personalisable form, to all those who want to discuss the details of their tax notice with her. La is not just a machine. She also appears as the outcome of the millions of interactions between the city, its infrastructure and its citizens.

Two lessons can be retained from this tale, which frequently flirts with philosophical storytelling. The first relates to the emergence of a more and more individualised relationship – one might almost describe it as intimate – between humankind and the city. Numerous mobile apps seek to promote such a relationship. The American city of Boston thus put in place an app called 'Citizens Connect', as of 2009, which allows its residents to indicate problems with public areas to the municipal authorities, such as damaged paving or a defective traffic signal.[11] For its part, the French telecommunications operator Orange is developing an experiment called 'Ma Ville Dans Ma Poche' with the city council of Bordeaux, which will offer residents a single portal to access a whole series of administrative services, as well as businesses and leisure facilities.[12]

Above all, the city no longer appears solely as a collection of technological infrastructure, spatial sequences, individuals and groups that is considered to be equipped with a personality in a metaphorical sense alone, or through an idealisation that is often tainted by political preoccupations. Take for example Charles de Gaulle's famous 'Paris! Paris outraged! Paris broken! Paris martyred! But Paris liberated!' speech, which he gave on the occasion of the French capital's liberation from Nazi occupation.[13] On this point, Haldeman's scenario is similar to the visions of digital theoreticians, designers and artists who have proved themselves less cautious than the majority of urban specialists.[14]

Of course, science fiction is no longer necessarily the most favoured means for inventing the future. As the French digital media specialist Nicolas Nova pointed out in an essay on the limitations of this long-dominant genre, today the future is sketched out perhaps more through a mixture of technological anticipation and everyday reality than through novels, short stories and films that straddle centuries and take the reader on a voyage from planet to planet.[15] But is it really all that crucial to know whether such a mixture between techno-futures and the everyday still stems from the typical language of science fiction? It is perhaps more essential to observe the irreplaceable role that has been allocated to the imagination and all sorts of narratives in the development of information and communications technology. These narratives, whatever their status, need to be taken seriously. They convey expectations and desires that constitute, more than in other domains, one of the driving forces behind innovation. Because it infiltrates everyday life and social relationships much more than traditional technologies have done, digital technology involves desire as well as the narratives that shape it. The latter dictate the direction it takes as well as the objectives that are assigned to it. In other words, the fictional universe that develops around and about digital technology possesses a strongly self-fulfilling character. In the case of the smart city, it allows in particular the adjustment of its two dimensions: the ideal, and the concrete process of transformation.

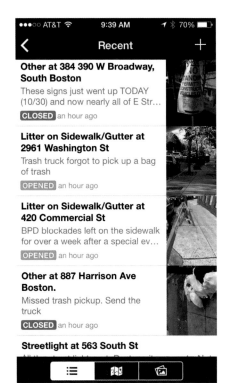

Screenshot of the 'Citizens Connect' application developed for the City of Boston, Massachusetts, 2015 Through this type of application designed for smartphones, citizens can experience a more personalised relationship to municipal services and contribute to the welfare of their city.

The development of ubiquitous computing is perhaps one of the best illustrations of this self-fulfilling character. This objective for computing to be at once omnipresent and invisible emerged in the early 1990s through visionary writings, such as the article by Mark Weiser, who was then director of the IT research centre at Xerox Palo Alto in California, on the 21st-century computer in the journal *Scientific American*.[16] This article, which was quickly followed by a whole series of publications on the same theme by Weiser and other major players in the field of computing, contributed to the launch of a genuine programme of research and development.[17] The latter varied widely and took on different names from one company to another: 'ambient intelligence' at Philips, whose terminology was taken up by the European Commission; 'pervasive computing' at IBM and Siemens. The programme was effective in many respects. Powers of calculation and digital resources are no longer confined to computers. They can now be found all over the place: in the numerous electronic chips that control the machines that surround us, in our household appliances, our cars, our mobile phones, our tablets, and soon in the networked eyewear and watches that firms such as Google and Apple are seeking to put on the market.[18] There are currently more than 50 billion connected devices sending data online. Created by the technology firm Umbrellium, the search engine 'Thingful' provides arresting maps displaying the localisation of some of the elements of what is often referred to as the 'Internet of Things'.[19]

Mark Weiser's article is not only interesting for its content, which announces evolutions that were still in embryonic form at the time, from the spread of Wi-Fi to the use of tactile tablets. It is also interesting for its form. It deliberately mixes the language of the manifesto with that of the research report. On the manifesto side, the most frequently quoted section is the incisive opening statement: 'The most profound technologies are those that disappear. They weave themselves into the fabric of everyday life until they are indistinguishable from it.'[20] On the research report side, the article goes through all sorts of innovations – from the electronic badge, to the tablet, to the programmable screen. But perhaps the most significant element, and the one which delivers the key to Weiser's intentions, lies in the description at the end of the article of the daily routine of Sal, a mother who works in Silicon Valley. As soon as she leaps out of bed, Sal can drink the coffee that her machine has prepared for her, having been warned of her imminent awakening by the

**Pervasive computing according to Siemens, 2004**
The proliferation of connected devices is among the consequences of the development of ubiquitous or pervasive computing. It allows objects such as bulletin boards to exchange information with mobile devices such as smartphones and tablets.

clock on her bedside table which recognises the preliminary signs that she is stirring. When she arrives at work, a screen indicates the available parking spaces. A little later, she corrects a text in the company of a colleague whose face is projected onto a screen on her wall. Her whole day is thus spent interacting with machines of varying size and function, which keep her informed, suggest how she should behave, and propose alternatives when her choices prove unwise. A recourse to fiction – a fiction mixing the everyday with technological innovations that were still surprising at the time – thus completes the demonstration, or rather summarises it.

According to the famous statement of another computer scientist who spent time at Xerox Palo Alto, Alan Curtis Kay, 'the best way to predict the future is to invent it'.[21] Since the beginnings of digital technology, fiction has played a particularly important role in this process of invention. In many cases, the narrative of future innovations is due to the computer scientists themselves. But novelists, scriptwriters and film directors have equally contributed to the formulation of some of the targets that have been set. Cyberspace thus owes something to the intuition of the writers William Gibson and Neal Stephenson, or rather it is part of the same metanarrative concerning the possibility of an online life which could

**An early Google Glass prototype, 2011**
Despite the lukewarm reception of the Google Glass, wearable computing devices are among the most promising directions of development of ubiquitous computing. In the near future, traditional screens may lose their hegemonic position as interfaces with the online world.

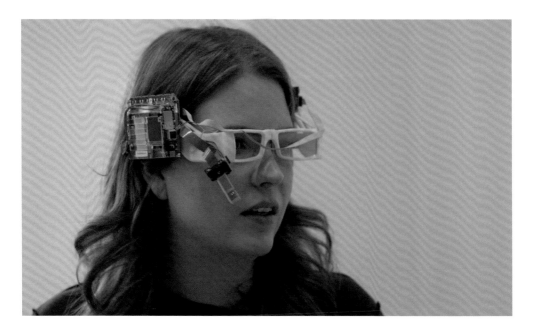

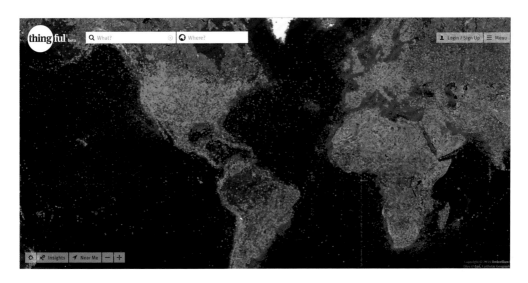

**Screenshot of the 'Thingful' search engine, 2015**
On 'Thingful' you can search the Internet of Things by locations, types of connected objects and ownership. With the proliferation of such objects, which are often wirelessly connected, the Internet is becoming both more and more spatially present and marked by the rise of people-to-machine and machine-to-machine communication.

absorb most of the energy from those willing to immerse themselves in its glittering, unpredictable fabric in the manner of a giant Las Vegas Strip.[22] The links between films such as *Minority Report* (2002) and innovations such as tactile interfaces, retinal scanners and augmented reality are well known. It is true that the aforementioned film's director, Steven Spielberg, had consulted all sorts of specialists in information and communications technology when preparing it. Digital technology feeds on fictions which possess a strongly self-fulfilling character.

As the Canadian communication specialist Vincent Mosco has emphasised, such fictions hark back to a number of founding myths, such as the abolition of space or the ideal of a technology that is both omnipresent and invisible, of which Mark Weiser ultimately did no more than to produce a new version.[23] But these myths alone cannot have generated the profusion of stories that are both similar and different and which lead to predicting the future through inventing it. The very particular relationship between the digital and the imaginary, or fiction, could well be explained by some of its fundamental characteristics. Its intimate relationship with communications must naturally be called into play. But it is its capacity to transform the everyday according to our desires that is again the most determining factor. Most self-fulfilling narratives, beginning with Mark Weiser's, emerge at the intersection of these two dimensions: communications and the everyday. Besides mundane tasks such as preparing breakfast or driving to work, digital-era activities involving communication or consulting new media punctuate Sal's day. The same ingredients are found in an evocation of the daily life of a group of residents of a smart city in the year 2050, which appeared a few years ago in *The Guardian*.[24]

The emergence of a form of non-human intelligence invested with functions of control and regulation is one of the founding myths of the digital era. This myth is for instance one of the driving forces behind the screenplay of Stanley Kubrick's *2001: A Space Odyssey* (1968). But the smart cities that are the subject of so many narratives today – from science-fiction novels like *The Accidental Time Machine*, to the business scenarios of IT companies like Cisco Systems and IBM, to articles in the daily press – are not intended to resemble the HAL 9000 computer which coordinates the space mission to Jupiter in Kubrick's film. And that is just as well, given that HAL's psychological vulnerability leads the mission with which it is entrusted into catastrophe!

Unlike the Big Brother-type centralised electronic brains of 1960s and 1970s science fiction, what are now being imagined are much more complex forms of intelligence. The analogy with giant centralised computers has been replaced by other models – the cyborg, the network and indeed the swarm – for reasons that have at least as much to do

Captain John Anderton, played by actor Tom Cruise, using a tactile interface in Steven Spielberg's *Minority Report*, 2002
*Minority Report* is typical of the strong relationship between fiction and the development of cutting-edge digital technologies. The self-fulfilling nature of these technologies is to a large extent responsible for these relationships.

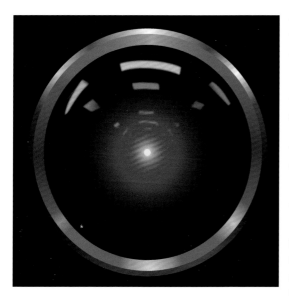

with the range of available technologies as with sociotechnical imagination. This state of available technologies needs to be brought in alongside the self-fulfilling character of narratives relating to the smart city. Although the smart city, in its most ambitious version, seems still to be a distant ideal, the process leading to it is already well under way. From this point of view, we might consider that we are already living in smart cities.

## The Sentient and Sensory City

Before turning to the subject of intelligence, we should perhaps start by bringing in the new capacity of cities to detect, measure and record what is happening within them

The 'eye' of the HAL 9000 computer in Stanley Kubrick's *2001: A Space Odyssey*, 1968
The red camera eye of HAL (for Heuristically programmed ALgorithmic computer) remains to this day one of the most powerful images of the seduction and dangers of artificial intelligence. In the case of smart cities, such a centralised system has relatively little chance of being implemented, despite the strong neocybernetic stance of some of those involved in their development.

– in technical networks as well as in streets and buildings, and in people's homes as well as in the offices of public administrative bodies. Sometimes visible, but more often hidden, countless chips and sensors allow objects and vehicles to be located, consumption levels and transactions to be recorded, and temperatures, pollution levels, population densities and flows to be measured.[25] In the Spanish city of Santander, for instance, there are some 20,000 sensors for 180,000 inhabitants, monitoring parameters such as temperature, luminosity, ground humidity and available parking slots.[26] Paris's 120,000 trees have each been fitted with a radio-frequency identification (RFID) chip, which allows the technicians responsible for parks and gardens to know their history and keep track of the interventions they have received. Again in Paris, the water consumption of individual apartment blocks is read remotely by the municipal agency in charge of supplying the capital. This allows Eau de Paris to identify leaks in the system more easily and to alert its clients in case of excessive consumption. In a large number of towns, vehicular traffic is monitored in real time through technology ranging from induction loops that allow the passage of vehicles to be noted, to wireless sensors, to video cameras. In Singapore, this monitoring enabled the introduction of one of the first dynamic pricing systems, which consists of making drivers pay in proportion to the desirability and, more importantly, the congestion levels of the thoroughfares they use. In the longer term, it is possible to envisage cities where automated driving is imposed, to improve traffic efficiency even further. Google Cars can already go driverless, and several US states have authorised their use on public roads.

More and more information is produced by urban dwellers themselves, whether by using smart travelcards like London's Oyster, Paris's Navigo or Tokyo's Suica, or by paying for their purchases with credit cards or mobile phones. From one year to the next, their activities and the information gathered about them are being monitored more intensely and above all more widely, in a constant to-ing and fro-ing between experiments and large-scale implementation policies. While their movements, their purchases and their consumption of water, gas and electricity have already been being recorded for a long time, attention is now also being paid to the waste that they are producing. With a view to improving household waste management, the SENSEable City Lab at MIT has thus monitored the circuit of waste produced in Seattle, from aluminium cans to plastic wrapping, identifying them through electronic chips.[27] The city of Seoul in South Korea has meanwhile launched an ambitious programme that consists of making its residents pay for their rubbish to be collected according to the quantity they have produced, through the use of RFID technology. The system notably involves rubbish bins that bill their users on a pro-rata basis, according to the weight of the waste they put into them.[28]

**Electronic road pricing gantry in Singapore, 2005**
Road pricing to regulate automobile traffic in congested metropolises has become common. In Singapore, vehicles are identified by an electronic device known as an In-vehicle Unit. In Stockholm, where a congestion tax has been implemented permanently since 2007, identification is based on automatic number-plate recognition.

**Google self-driving car prototype, 2014**
The future of urban automobile circulation could very well lie in the development of automatic vehicles like those tested by Google.

Cities are inexorably transforming themselves into information systems, with information often available in real time. Within these systems, relationships between physical infrastructure, service offers and users are being reconfigured, to work towards improved reactivity and greater flexibility of use. In many cases, the ultimate aim is better optimisation of scarce resources such as parking. For example, from San Francisco to Nice, a whole series of cities are trialling 'smart' parking systems in which sensors allow drivers to be informed of available parking spaces near their current location.[29] However, the main objective of the smart city is the quest for improved environmental efficiency, whether that be through reducing its energy consumption or the volume of waste it generates. This is the justification used by EDF, France's foremost electricity supply company, for the introduction of its Linky meter, which represents a first step towards more intelligent management of electrical supply and demand.

One of the key issues at the heart of this atmosphere of rapidly expanding urban information consists in being able to associate and, if possible, combine different types of measurements and recordings. With this in mind, the city of Nice, in collaboration with Cisco Systems, launched an experiment for a 'connected boulevard' where various sensors collect real-time data on traffic circulation, street lighting, environmental quality and cleanliness. The aim was to create a shared information platform allowing both administrative bodies and private developers to offer innovative

services at the interface between the physical and digital worlds.[30] These integration perspectives can be found in major projects for new smart cities where the emphasis is simultaneously on sustainable development and digital technology, such as Masdar and Songdo. Behind these flagship projects, it must nevertheless be admitted that many plans for developing urban intelligence are still lacking in coherence, and seem to have come from a catalogue of separate initiatives that are as yet rather poorly co-ordinated. The digital strategy proclaimed by the French city of Lyons, among other examples, mixes together very different themes – encouraging energy transition, proposing new mobility solutions, aiding business creation – while seldom making clear how they may be linked.[31] This undoubtedly stems from what is still the very experimental character of many developments. It is as though this were the time for expansion, rather than for the consolidation that is nevertheless necessary once a certain stage has been reached.

There are many more examples of 'smart' experiments and achievements. They rely on the capacity to detect and record, often in real time, what is going on in the urban grid. In a certain number of cases, these recordings can directly generate instructions for the automatic control of technical infrastructures, in the manner of thermostats and other temperature

SENSEable City Lab, MIT, 'Trash Track' project, Seattle, 2009
The experiment led by the SENSEable City Lab reveals the sometimes extremely complex itineraries of discarded objects on their way to recycling or final disposal. It contributes to the development of a new field of research on how to improve the ecological footprint of cities.

controllers like the Nest thermostat that adapts dynamically to the behaviour of its users.[32] Sensors are then paired with activators responsible for initiating the execution of such instructions. In this sort of situation, it is hard to see in what way the city is truly becoming more intelligent than the great regulated technical systems that have already existed for quite some time. But automatic control is a long way from exhausting the range of possible scenarios. In a whole series of other cases, the aim is to inform operators and/or users by proposing a range of choices and allowing them to understand the consequences of each.

Operators and/or users: the distinction between these two categories of stakeholders is becoming more and more hazy in the context of the smart city. This is a rather widespread characteristic in the digital realm. As many commentators have noted, Web 2.0 has blurred the old dividing line between amateurs and professionals.[33] There is no such differentiation on Wikipedia, for example. Similarly, the application of information and communications technology to the city, with a view to making it more sustainable, demands increasing investment on the part of users, who are called to become ever more closely associated with the management of the new services that are offered to them. In smart grids, the new networks of energy production and distribution that are claimed to be intelligent, the final users are taking a growing role – whether they are likely to influence the energy offer, if they are producing hydraulic, solar or wind power themselves, or the demand, by keeping a closer eye on their consumption than before. This is one of the objectives of the new Linky meter. The same ambition was at the origin of the Green Button Initiative launched in 2012 in the United States in order to provide utility customers with data regarding their energy usage.[34] Recycling of household waste likewise relies

**Smart food waste disposal in Daegu, Susenggu, South Korea, 2015**
With these food disposal units similar to those tested in Seoul, each user of the system pays according to the disposal costs of their food waste. Besides financial fairness, the aim is to make citizens feel more responsible for their behaviour and its impact on the environment.

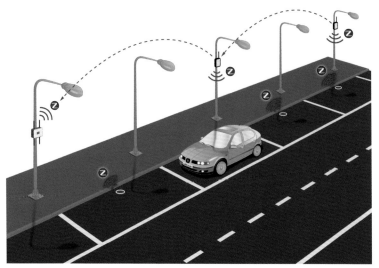

Smart parking sensor platform devised by Libelium, 2011
Sensors buried in parking spaces detect the arrival and departure of vehicles. The information is conveyed to system integrators to offer comprehensive parking management solutions.

on massive investment from individuals. From energy management to waste treatment, city dwellers are more and more frequently finding themselves called to action and faced with strategic choices that affect the overall balance of technical systems. A new model of consumer is emerging which is blurring the traditional line between operators and users.

The consequence of this set of developments resides in the fact that an increasing number of individuals have access to real-time information on their city, a city in which they can control certain functions. This information and control can be brought about through various means. On this subject, the growing role of smartphones – the mobile screens that are assisting us ever more frequently and with ever more diverse tasks, espousing some of our desires especially closely – should be noted. In 2014, around 60 per cent of mobile phone owners in the United States possessed a

Installation of a smart electricity meter in France, 2011
Linky, the meter promoted by EDF, France's foremost electricity supply company, is intended as a first step towards a better management of the electricity grid.

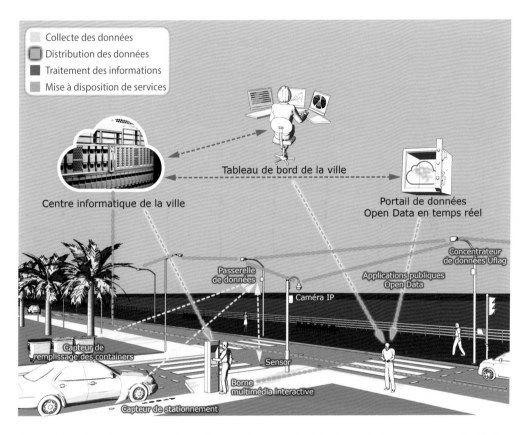

Collecte des données
Distribution des données
Traitement des informations
Mise à disposition de services

Tableau de bord de la ville

Centre informatique de la ville

Portail de données
Open Data en temps réel

Concentrateur
de données Uflag

Passerelle
de données

Applications publiques
Open Data

Caméra IP

Capteur de
remplissage des containers

Sensor

Borne
multimédia interactive

Capteur de stationnement

**Connected boulevard project in Nice, France, developed with Cisco Systems, 2013**
The data collected on the boulevard are sent to the city computing centre (the cloud on the left), before being displayed on the city dashboard (figure in the centre). They also feed an open data portal (on the right).

smartphone.[35] The 50-per-cent level had already been reached in the EU5 countries (UK, Germany, France, Spain and Italy) by the end of the year 2012.[36] This market penetration is not restricted to developed countries. During 2013, the proportion of smartphones rose from 10 per cent to more than 22 per cent of the total number of mobile phones in India, and this growth is forecast to continue at a sustained pace in 2014–15.[37] Even more than the 'fifth screen' – the electronic bulletin board that many towns are still counting on to improve their communication – it is the smartphone screen that is currently making the most difference to our relationship with the city.[38] All kinds of information relating to the environment, transport and cultural life are displayed on it in real time. It can also be used to decipher the two-dimensional barcodes that are proliferating all over the place on urban walls.

Through the various terminals which city residents can access to inform themselves and make decisions – mobile phones being foremost among them – something like a dawning of city consciousness is being brought about, in which the city discovers the state it is in as well as the directions it may take. Revealingly, the municipality of the highly connected city of Santander runs a website called 'Santander City Brain' to collect ideas and suggestions about its present state and future.[39] The impression of a dawning consciousness is at the origin of the notion of the sentient city, which has aroused the interest of numerous researchers, designers and artists.[40] It is as though the urban realm were suddenly equipped with a sensitivity capable of resulting in some form of consciousness, or even self-awareness.

Although there is not strictly a relationship of cause and effect between these two sequences of phenomena, but rather a shared source – the individual in the digital era (which will be discussed in chapter 2) – the intuition of a city that has developed the equivalent of sensations is reinforced by the prominence of the senses: sight, but also hearing, smell, taste and even touch, as much in the way we represent the city as in the judgements we make about it. Tactility in particular constitutes a rapidly rising dimension in contemporary culture. This is witnessed by the new place accorded to it by architecture through what tends to be described as the 'return' of ornament.[41] Before the sentient city, or rather as a complement to the capacity of feeling that we attribute to it, stands an individual who, far from being cut off from sensation by the digital revolution, reveals him- or herself to be hyper-receptive to all types of sensory stimuli. There have been many publications by researchers and critics examining the consequences of this hyper-receptivity in fields from contemporary art to gastronomy.[42] As for the city of senses, the sensory city or indeed the sensual city, in 2005–6 the Canadian Centre for Architecture dedicated an exhibition to the theme which revealed the new urban issues that are attached to it.[43] The subject went on to become the main theme of the French contribution to the 2010 Shanghai Expo coordinated by the architect Jacques Ferrier.[44]

Sentient city and sensory or even sensual city: the two perspectives are interrelated. The notion of the senseable city, to which the laboratory founded by Carlo Ratti at MIT refers, purposely plays on the confusion between these two possible interpretations of the urban realm in order to propose a city that would be at once equipped with some form of sensibility and detectable through the senses, with or without the assistance of information and communications tools (sensors).[45] Furthermore, both

Herzog & de Meuron, de Young Museum, San Francisco, 2003
Typical of the 'return of ornament' in architecture, the envelope of the museum seems to blur the boundary between sight and touch with its dots that evoke the Braille alphabet.

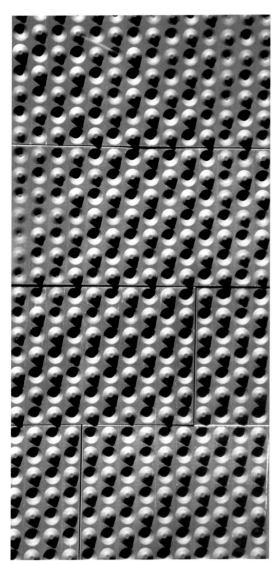

refer to development issues that are related to the digital. This is obvious in the case of the sentient city, as already discussed. For its part, the sensory or sensual city reveals itself as inseparable from the aspirations of the 'creative class', to adopt an expression of the American urban studies theorist Richard Florida, which is at the origin of this new knowledge economy founded on the digital that is presented as an alternative to traditional development scenarios.[46] The stakeholders who embody this new mode of development, be they scientists, businesspeople or designers, are striving for a rich and varied urban environment that engages all five senses. Art galleries, performance venues, gastronomic restaurants and fashion boutiques all pertain to the ecology that the knowledge economy requires, just as much as sensors, fibre optics and ubiquitous computing do. Their absence around Kendall Square, in the business district developed by MIT at the gates of its campus, is seen by the institution as a problem that needs to be resolved as quickly as possible.[47] There can be no lasting intelligent growth without a stimulating urban environment.

Despite this type of relationship, the hypothesis of the sentient city, an urban organism capable of feeling and of accessing some form of consciousness, or even self-awareness, remains far harder to comprehend than that of the sensory or sensual city. It essentially leads back to the question of the smart city that is at the foundation of this book. Intelligent, yes; but in which sense? Before at last addressing this question directly, let us continue to gather clues, paying particular attention to two other dimensions of the sentient city: first of all the accumulation of data relating to it, and then the importance of the occurrences and events that punctuate its life.

UNStudio, Galleria
Department Store facade,
Seoul, South Korea, 2004
Another instance of the
return of ornament in
architecture. The changing
colours of the glass discs
of this facade respond
to the dynamics of
atmospheric conditions.
They are intended to induce
pleasurable sensations in the
passers-by and shoppers.

## Massive Quantities of Data

One of the direct consequences of the proliferation of chips and
sensors is a massive accumulation of data relating to the city and how
it functions. Mobile phones alone supply large quantities of information
about, for example, their owners' locations and the calls they make. With
smartphones, which allow access to the Internet, even greater quantities
of data can be collected. More generally, cities are progressively entering

**Office dA, BanQ restaurant, Boston, Massachusetts, 2008**
Gastronomy represents an essential dimension of the smart city. High-end restaurants have become strategic assets in the competition to attract members of the 'creative class' in order to promote a knowledge-based urban economy.

a new phase in their development that is marked by exponential growth in the production and storage of information. At the same time, the strategic character of the urban realm is intensifying for a whole range of big businesses, since information seems more and more to be the strategic resource that drives the engine of capitalism. Being present in such a market cannot be justified solely by the direct profit generated by the sale of products and services. It also allows access to a precious data set that can be either directly exploited or sold on.

In such a perspective, the question of the control of information produced by cities arises immediately. On this point, the diversity of existing attitudes is obvious. While some municipal authorities seek to maintain control of the data generated by urban services, others seem strangely indifferent to this issue. The fact that the question has only recently emerged may explain the latters' indifference at least in part. It would be fair to wager that this will have been banished in a few years' time, when the question of information ownership will be unavoidable and will represent a major political challenge.

Also related to this is the difficulty cities have in acquiring coherent strategies in a field where everything moves too quickly – so much so that it is perhaps impossible to build a stable outlook.

Besides ownership, accessibility represents another sizeable issue. Who has the right to consult and use the data? It should be noted here that rights are not the only aspect of accessibility; it also brings up technical questions of formatting and readability. It is possible to have the theoretical right to consult information but to be unable to read it for the lack of technical training or appropriate software. Only a tiny minority of users are capable of exploiting the raw data that are produced by the smart city's various sensors and servers. The rest need them to be formatted so that they can read and interpret them. The increasingly strategic character of urban mapping, which is intended to render the information produced by cities visible, should be considered in this perspective. The map constitutes one of the ways to make the ideal of open data – which is demanded by a whole range of stakeholders, municipal authorities, Townsend-type civic hackers and community activists – effective. Making data produced by cities available to all would seem to be a new citizens' objective.[48] But, upstream from the statistics and maps that are delivered to the public, do not the formatting of

**Elkus Manfredi Architects, image of an 'active street', 2013**
The image was used by MIT during a zoning petition. It is not intended to represent actual building designs but to convey the overall ambience of the new Kendall Square district. Numerous shops, cafés and restaurants contribute to the animation of the street.

data and the writing of interfaces that allow them to be read and interpreted, a genuine predigestion of information, confer excessive power on those who are responsible for them? As with data ownership, the way we choose to make data accessible gives rise to questions of a political nature that are only partly answered by the current discourse on the public character of data.

In literature relating to big data, these issues are often relegated to the background by the prospect of achieving a new science of cities based on correlations that would not previously have been noticed between apparently unconnected phenomena, as well as on a more thorough and, above all, more realistic modelling of urban functioning, which is often described, with reference to living organisms, as metabolism. Some enthusiasts' writings can give the impression that the data will spontaneously generate new knowledge, in the manner of an archive that no longer needs historians to produce information about the objects contained within it. While it is of course possible to imagine that algorithms might one day take over from humans to exploit the massive quantities of information that cities are creating, it seems more feasible to envisage a cooperation between machines and humans, even if only to interpret the revealed correlations.

IBM, infographic on 'turning big data into insight', 2013
The document is part of a promotional campaign for IBM's SmartCloud and Smarter Cities Intelligent Operations software. One of the objectives of the latter is to provide a dashboard that enables better decisions to be made for cities by tapping into big data. Such an ambition carries with it a distinct neocybernetic connotation.

# Smarter Cities: Turning Big Data Into Insight

## City Planning and Operations

**$1 Trillion**
global annual savings could be attained by optimizing public infrastructure.
Source: McKinsey

**$57 Trillion**
in infrastructure investments will be needed between 2013-2030.
Source: McKinsey

## Transportation Analytics

**50 Hours**
of traffic delays per year are incurred, on average, by travelers.

**30 Billion**
people all over the world travel approximately 30 billion miles per year. By 2050, that figure will grow to over 150 billion miles.

Cloud is driving cities in their digital transformation.

## Water Management

**60%**
of water allocated for domestic human use goes to urban cities.

**$14 Billion**
in potable water is lost every year because of leaks, theft and unbilled usage.
Source: World Bank

**37,000**
cloud experts support IBM's industry team alone.

## Open Cloud

**$6 Billion**
has been invested by IBM in more than a dozen acquisitions to accelerate its cloud initiatives.

IBM Intelligent Operations software is designed with cities, for cities, to provide the tools to monitor, visualize and analyze vital city services such as water and wastewater systems, transportation, infrastructure planning, permit management and emergency response.

In the meantime, it is an illusion to believe that pertinent questions emerge of their own accord, like fungus on the compost of big data. Modelling optimism meanwhile reflects what is perhaps another illusion: that of the city as a system which, while not closed in on itself, is driven only by a finite number of parameters. Such an illusion already typified the systemically and cybernetics-inspired attempts at urban modelling of the 1950s and 1960s, such as the 'urban dynamics' developed by the American computer engineer and systems scientist Jay Forrester in the late 1960s.[49] In this respect it is revealing to see Forrester included among the pioneers frequently mentioned today in literature on smart cities. He features for example among the sources consulted by IBM researchers who were seeking to establish a general theory of the smart city, as well as among those used in a 2013 book on urban modelling that is revealingly entitled *The New Science of Cities*, published by the British urbanist and educator Michael Batty.[50]

This return of the temptation to consider the city as a system founded on a feedback loop between parameters that are finite in number touches on one of the foundational elements of this neocybernetic approach to

Joan Serras and James Cheshire, 'Mapped: Every-day Bus Trips in London', 2012
This map shows the 114,000 daily bus trips in London. The wider and redder the lines, the more buses running along them. Timetable data from over 22,000 London bus stops were used to create a representation emblematic of the new type of urban visualisation made possible by using a very large data set.

Jay Forrester, 'Life cycle of
an urban area – 250 years
of internal development,
maturity, and stagnation',
1969
Jay Forrester's *Urban
Dynamics* (MIT Press
(Cambridge, MA), 1969) was
among the first ambitious
attempts to model urban
evolution over the long term.
Some of the conclusions
reached by Forrester, such
as the damaging effect of
building low-cost housing,
proved highly controversial.
Equally unappealing for
many was the prospect of
long-term urban stagnation.
For its author, these
somewhat counterintuitive
results proved the fecundity
of urban modelling, a belief
shared by many proponents
of big data mining.

intelligence, which will be discussed further in the following chapter. Such an approach also refers to an even more fundamental shift, in the final stage of which events and occurrences tend to occupy an ever more determining position in the urban experience as well as in the management of cities. While the networked city that progressively emerged with the industrial era accorded absolute priority to flow management, the latter often tends to fade into the background behind the perception of the dense web of events that take place in cities and the plan to control their evolution in order to construct ideal development scenarios.[51] Flows themselves are more and more systematically perceived from the viewpoint of the events that give them rhythm or disrupt that rhythm. To convince ourselves of this, we need only think of the increasingly determining role that is played by traffic jams and accidents in the perception of vehicular circulation. Like the smart city, the networked city appeared as both an ideal and a concrete process of transformation. This ideal and process are now being replaced. The advent of a new urban intelligence is leading to the transition from the networked city to the event-city.

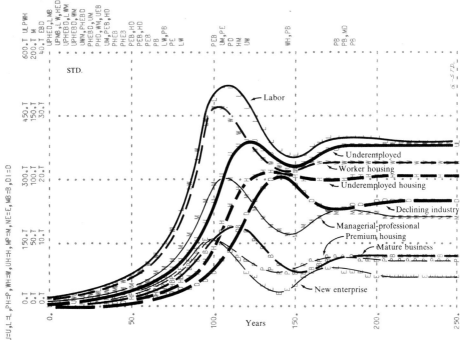

**Figure 1-1** Life cycle of an urban area—250 years of internal development, maturity, and stagnation.

## What Happens

On the screens to which they connect themselves, city dwellers have access to occurrences, events and situations, rather than to physical 'things', objects and organisations. Certainly, street layouts are displayed on smartphone screens, but above all what are presented to view are the place where the phone's owner is located and the possibilities at his or her disposal. Occurrences and events: such are also the state of traffic and the existence of jams, the detection of a breakdown or online purchases by consumers who identify themselves through the use of passwords. More widely, every day the sensors and meters of the smart city record millions of elementary occurrences, the temperature at such and such a place, the presence or lack of vehicles, and water and electricity consumption. These

Jean-Charles Alphand, map of the sewers of Paris on 1 January 1889, *Les travaux de Paris 1789–1889*, Paris, 1889
More than any other 19th-century metropolis, the new Paris planned and built by Haussmann and his engineers appears as a networked city where flow management played an essential role.

micro-occurrences agglomerate to reveal more general situations. Traffic maps such as the ones offered by the Sytadin system for the Île-de-France region around Paris are typical of the results that are obtained at the culmination of this agglomeration process. In the minds of its connected citizens, the city begins to merge with everything that is going on within it.

The French philosopher and urbanist Paul Virilio has suspected this event-based character for some time. It formed the theme of an exhibition and book supported by the Fondation Cartier in 2002–3, entitled *Ce Qui Arrive*, meaning 'what happens', in its original French version (though its official English title was *Unknown Quantity*).[52] In Virilio's eyes, the theme necessarily took on a catastrophic tone, from ecological accidents to terrorist attacks such as those of 11 September 2001. Behind these apocalyptic scenarios, cities tend to appear more and more as systems of occurrences and events that sometimes agglomerate and sometimes fit one inside the other. In the first case, the result is overall situations, as has just been explained; in the second, it is the events that now punctuate the lives

**Screenshot of the Sytadin website at 2:45 pm on 22 January 2015**
Sytadin offers real-time traffic information on Paris and its region. It signals ongoing roadworks and accidents.

of medium-sized towns as well as metropolises – calendars of sporting, festive and political occasions – and whose importance in the definition of the city is only on the increase. Related to this evolution, the iconic monuments of cultural capitals equally tend to be assimilated into events. The Eiffel Tower no longer constitutes so much a 300-metre-high metal structure erected in the 19th century as a constantly renewed celebration of Parisian identity in which tourists are invited to participate. Its visitor numbers – 6.7 million in 2013 – likewise represent a situation constructed from micro-occurrences which are meticulously tracked by the organisation in charge of managing the Tower.[53]

Piled up, agglomerated, fitted one inside the other or – more often than not – all in a tangled muddle, occurrences, events and situations form the threads from which the fabric of today's great urban narratives are woven. Even more than urbanists' plans, it is the narratives and scenarios that are inspired by them which allow cities to set objectives for themselves. The often-denounced crisis of urban planning is revealed to be contemporary with the rise in power of an event-based city in which reality and fiction are often difficult to distinguish from each other. For example, it is possible to pass almost imperceptibly from the visitor numbers for the Eiffel Tower and events such as 'Paris Plages', for which temporary artificial beaches are created along the river Seine in summer, to the narrative of Paris as tourist capital of Europe, or even of the world,

Cover of Paul Virilio's *Ce qui arrive*, Actes Sud (Arles), 2002
In the exhibition and catalogue entitled *Ce qui arrive* (literally 'what happens'), Virilio developed an interpretation of the contemporary city based on the importance attached to devastating events such as accidents, ecological catastrophes and terrorist attacks. The public paid particular attention to this interpretation, in the immediate aftermath of the 11 September attacks of 2001.

Cargo plane crash in
Amsterdam, Netherlands,
4 October 1992
The crash of a cargo
plane belonging to the
Israeli airline El Al on the
Bijlmermeer neighbourhood
of Amsterdam killed 43
people. Because of its
spectacular character, the
accident was among those
referred to by Virilio in *Ce
qui arrive*.

which constitutes one of the clearly declared strategies of Paris's municipal
authority. Despite the publication from time to time of regional-scale
masterplans, the French state's 'Grand Paris' initiative, launched in 2007 to
adapt the metropolis and fit it for the 21st century, also stems more from
narrative than from traditional planning. It revels in successful substories,
such as that of the Saclay plateau south of the city, which has been dubbed
the European Silicon Valley or France's Cambridge, Massachusetts. The plan
for the regional metro system's development up to 2050 also seems to
come straight out of fiction – a fiction to which it is tempting to attribute
a self-fulfilling character, on the model of what happened in the field of
information and communications technology.[54]

Paris is not the only metropolis to feed off self-fulfilling narratives. The event-
city par excellence, with its half-million surveillance cameras, royal news
updates and Olympic Games, London dreams of bristling with crystal towers
like those of Shanghai. It aspires to reconcile Asian-style economic dynamism
with European-style sustainable development.

However, beyond the ticket offices of Parisian monuments and the surveillance
cameras of London, the role played by digital technology in the rise of the

event-city stems from something more fundamental than the omnipresence
of instruments for capturing what is happening. Information possesses, by its
very definition, an event-based character, since it corresponds to the selection
of a given state within a range of possible states. This begins with the basic bit
of information which, as is well known, can take a value of 0 or 1 – the value
finally taken appearing as a micro-occurrence. The French philosopher Pierre
Lévy put it well when he wrote that: 'a bit is neither a particle of matter, nor
an element of an idea, it is an atom of circumstance'.[55]

Ever since the very beginning, the world that information and
communications technology has been helping to bring about has possessed
a strongly event-based character. It is no accident that one of the first major
computer networks, and the first where something could be revealed on
screens thanks to a computer, is related to the paroxysmic events that are
thermonuclear strikes. This is the Semi-Automatic Ground Environment
system, better known as SAGE: a set of tools for aircraft detection and anti-
aircraft defence to protect North America against possible attacks from the
Soviet Union, which was coordinated through the largest computers of the
period, built by IBM specially for the purpose.[56] At the height of the Cold War,
what could be seen on the screens in the SAGE system's control rooms were
events and situations – and these could be virtual or real, because the reign

of computer simulation began at the same time as the response plans for possible thermonuclear attacks were being developed.

It is interesting to note that the inventor of the SAGE system is the same Jay Forrester who is today recognised as one of the pioneers of urban simulation with his 'urban dynamics'. What is more, the city development scenarios that Forrester elaborated rely on the same type of program as the one that powered SAGE. From the outset, computer simulation has covered a vast area extending from defence problems to urban and even environmental issues, since Forrester's program was also to serve as a basis for the Club of Rome think-tank's scenarios in the early 1970s concerning the exhaustion of natural resources and the increase in pollution.[57]

With the rise of simulation, the boundary between what is really happening and what is simply likely to occur is becoming less clear than before. In envisioning a supercomputer, a distant descendant of those in the SAGE system, which can no longer quite tell the difference between simulated and real attacks (even though it controls the launch of the United States' intercontinental missiles), the film *WarGames*, directed by John Badham in 1983, reveals the risks of such a shift from the real to the virtual event. Although reality has always fed on fiction, the influence of the latter has been considerably reinforced with the advent of the digital.

**Factory Fifteen, a possible future skyline of London, 2011**
Other key elements of many London scenarios for the future include the strong presence of high-rise buildings that conjure up a European version of the Shanghai district of Pudong, as well as various elements of green infrastructure.

View of a control room of the SAGE system, 1959
On the screens of the SAGE system, one of the very first large-scale computer networks, operators could monitor events and situations related to the defence of North American airspace.

Revealingly, it is an adolescent video gamer who sparks off the crisis portrayed in *WarGames*, by hacking the website of the North American Aerospace Defense Command (NORAD) and setting about playing with the computer. Video games plunge their devotees into a universe dominated by occurrences, events and scenarios. While the settings contribute to the immersive character of each round, it is the events, quests and battles that matter most. The world of video games, where players pursue objectives and frequently take aim at other players, still today displays aggressive or even militaristic characteristics. It appears as the heir of some of the logics developed in the Cold War period – such as the importance of the human–machine pairing, which was to generate the theme of the cyborg, and the impossibility of completely distinguishing between reality and fiction. It was this impossibility that turned the Cold War into a 'game' where hypotheses were rife, and where scenarios managed to achieve as much importance as facts. Even more than the conflicts that preceded it, the Cold War went back to a series of grand narratives, or rather a metanarrative which justifies taking arms when faced by a potential worldwide conflict that must be avoided at any cost. Pending this inconceivable event, the metanarrative of a clash between blocs gives meaning to regional and local clashes and to the partial narratives that they generate, such as the countless stories relating to the Vietnam War. Here again, the video game takes on board this importance of the metanarrative, which serves as a background for the rounds in which the gamers engage.

Occurrences, events, situations and scenarios circulate from the city to the video game. The narrative dimension is another unifying factor between these realities that are otherwise so different. A strong social component might also be added to the list of possible analogies. Because – contrary to the vision of their detractors, who are quick to reduce them to a solitary exercise of reaction and adaptation skills – many online games, beginning with the famous *World of Warcraft* which brought together some 12 million gamers at its peak in 2010, are also platforms for socialising.

**The command centre of NORAD, still from John Badham's *WarGames*, 1983**
On the screens of the command centre, a nuclear war simulation game played between the NORAD mainframe and the main protagonist of the film, a high-school student who has hacked the NORAD computer network. Only the computer does not know the difference between simulation and reality.

Screenshot from the Ubisoft video game *Watch Dogs*, 2014
Aiden Pearce, the hero of the game, checking his smartphone. The smartphone is an essential component of the game. It enables Pearce to hack into various devices linked to the city's central operating system.

This set of analogies forms the stage onto which various games that use the space of the city as a setting invite themselves. Armed with their smartphones, participants carry out missions at the interface of the physical and digital worlds, immersed in this augmented reality that increasingly constitutes the framework of an urban experience in which atoms and bits would seem to be joining forces. The game *Watch Dogs*, launched in 2014 by Ubisoft, summons up this enriched urban experience by presenting a character who has to use his smartphone to survive in a futuristic Chicago. Does this mean that cities, as well as schools and businesses, are becoming 'gamified'? There is much talk of gamification in relation to the application of video-game logic to all sorts of areas, from education to services. Our perception of the city likewise carries the mark of this proliferation of gaming culture.

Like many of the fundamental aspects of human culture, the notion of the game has always been ambiguous. For example, how far is it appropriate to extend a notion that encompasses everything from children's games, chess and relaxation at no cost, to sporting competitions, World Cups and Olympic Games which may have considerable financial and political interests attached to them? Digital culture has amplified some of these ambiguities. 'Serious games', which go hand in hand with the rise of simulation, thus deliberately mingle the tone of entertainment with that of competition, allowing schools and businesses to refine their pupils' and employees' reflexes and to test new strategies. Above all, in many video games the true identity of those playing them is problematic. Surely the real protagonists are those who have conceived virtual worlds such as *World of Warcraft* and *Final Fantasy*, rather than those who come into conflict within them by following pre-established scenarios? As will be shown in chapter 2, this issue is not unrelated to some of the questions raised by the development of intelligent cities. Who should govern them: a caste of decision-makers who are likely to program the urban realm in the manner of a life-size game, or all those whose actions come together to make them into living environments? The transition from the city of flows to the city of events, situations and scenarios is accompanied by major political uncertainties.

# References

**1** IBM Smarter Cities Challenge, http://smartercitieschallenge.org/index.html (consulted 12 November 2014).

**2** ABI Research, '$39.5 Billion Will Be Spent on Smart City Technologies in 2016', https://www.abiresearch.com/press/395-billion-will-be-spent-on-smart-city-technologi (consulted 2 December 2014).

**3** Giulio Boccaletti, Markus Löffler and Jeremy M Oppenheim, 'How IT Can Cut Carbon Emissions', *McKinsey Quarterly*, October 2008, http://kyotoclub.org/docs/mckinsey_it_ott08.pdf (consulted 19 November 2014).

**4** Global e-Sustainability Initiative, *GeSI SMARTer 2020: The Role of ICT in Driving a Sustainable Future*, report of the Boston Consulting Group, December 2012, http://gesi.org/assets/js/lib/tinymce/jscripts/tiny_mce/plugins/ajaxfilemanager/uploaded/SMARTer%20 2020%20-%20The%20 Role%20of%20ICT%20 in%20Driving%20a%20 Sustainable%20Future%20 -%20December%202012._1. pdf (consulted 19 November

2014).

**5** Adam Greenfield, *Against the Smart City: A Pamphlet*, Verso (New York), 2013.

**6** Richard Sennett, 'No One Likes a City That's Too Smart', *The Guardian*, 4 December 2012, http://www.theguardian.com/commentisfree/2012/dec/04/smart-city-rio-songdo-masdar (consulted 21 November 2014).

**7** Rem Koolhaas, 'My Thoughts on the Smart City', edited transcript of a talk given at the High Level Group meeting on smart cities, Brussels, 24 September 2014, https://ec.europa.eu/commission_2010-2014/kroes/en/content/my-thoughts-smart-city-rem-koolhaas (consulted 24 November 2014).

**8** Thomas P Hughes, *Networks of Power: Electrification in Western Society 1880–1930*, Johns Hopkins University Press (Baltimore), 1983.

**9** Anthony M Townsend, *Smart Cities: Big Data, Civic Hackers, and the Quest for a New Utopia*, WW Norton & Company (New York and London), 2013.

**10** Joe W Haldeman, *The Accidental Time Machine*, Ace

Books (New York), 2007.

**11** Presentation of Citizens Connect, http://www.cityofboston.gov/doit/apps/citizensconnect.asp (consulted 29 December 2014).

**12** Presentation of the app 'Ma Ville Dans Ma Poche', http://www.orange.com/sirius/hello/2013/plus-loin-avec-les-nouveaux-usages/ma-ville-dans-ma-poche.html (consulted 26 November 2014).

**13** 'Paris! Paris outragé! Paris brisé! Paris martyrisé! mais Paris libéré!' Charles de Gaulle, speech given on 25 August 1944 at the Paris City Hall, http://www.charles-de-gaulle.org/pages/l-homme/accueil/discours/pendant-la-guerre-1940-1946/discours-de-l-hotel-de-ville-de-paris-25-aout-1944.php (consulted 26 November 2014).

**14** See for instance Mark Shepard (ed), *Sentient City: Ubiquitous Computing, Architecture, and the Future of Urban Space*, MIT Press (Cambridge, Massachusetts) and the Architectural League of New York (New York), 2011 and Valérie Châtelet (ed), *Anomalie Digital Arts*, no 6, 'Interactive Cities', HYX

(Orléans), February 2007.

15 Nicolas Nova, *Futurs? La Panne des imaginaires technologiques*, Les Moutons Electriques (Montélimar), 2014.

16 Mark Weiser, 'The Computer for the 21st Century', *Scientific American*, vol 265, no 3, September 1991, pp 94–104.

17 For a more recent version of this programme of research and development, see Adam Greenfield, *Everyware: The Dawning Age of Ubiquitous Computing*, New Riders (Berkeley, California), 2006.

18 Paul Dourish, Genevieve Bell, *Divining a Digital Future: Mess and Mythology in Ubiquitous Computing*, MIT Press (Cambridge, Massachusetts), 2011.

19 https://thingful.net/. See also Kat Austen, 'Thingful Site Brings Linked Internet of Things to Life', *New Scientist*, 18 December 2013, http://www.newscientist.com/article/dn24771-thingful-site-brings-linked-internet-of-things-to-life.html#.VLuYotE5C50 (consulted 18 January 2015).

20 Weiser 1991, p 94.

21 Alan Curtis Kay, 'Predicting the Future', *Stanford Engineering*, vol 1, no 1, Autumn 1989, pp 1–6, p 1 in particular.

22 William Gibson, *Neuromancer*, Ace Books (New York), 1984; Neal Stephenson, *Snow Crash* [1992], Bantam (New York), 2003.

23 Vincent Mosco, *The Digital Sublime: Myth, Power, and Cyberspace*, MIT Press (Cambridge, Massachusetts), 2004.

24 Michael Durham, 'Forty Years From Now … A Glimpse of How Daily Life Might Look in the Smartcity of 2050', *The Guardian*, http://www.guardian.co.uk/smarter-cities/forty-years-from-now (consulted 1 December 2014).

25 See for instance Fabien Eychenne, *La Ville 2.0, complexe … et familière*, FYP éditions (Limoges), 2008.

26 Delphine Cuny, 'Santander: la ville aux 20.000 capteurs, modèle du smart city européen', *La Tribune*, 7 November 2014, http://www.latribune.fr/technos-medias/internet/20141107tribe37bf8af2/santander-la-ville-aux-20-000-capteurs-modele-du-smart-city-europeen.html (consulted 18 January 2015).

27 SENSEable City Lab, 'Trash/Track', http://senseable.mit.edu/trashtrack/index.php (consulted 2 December 2014).

28 Nam Hyun-Woo, Baek Byung-Yeul and Park Ji-Won, 'More Food Waste, More Disposal Charges', *Korea Times*, 4 June 2013, http://www.koreatimes.co.kr/www/news/culture/2013/07/399_136904.html (consulted 2 December 2014).

29 Randall Stross, 'The Learning Curve of Smart Parking', *New York Times*, 22 December 2012, http://www.nytimes.com/2012/12/23/technology/smart-parking-has-a-learning-curve-too.html (consulted 2 December 2012); 'Nice équipe ses places de parking de capteurs intelligents', *Innov' in the City*, 16 January 2012, http://www.innovcity.fr/2012/01/16/nice-equipe-places-parking-capteurs-intelligents/ (consulted 2 December 2014).

30 Elsa Sidawy, 'Nice inaugure le premier boulevard "connecté" du monde', *Innov' in the City*, 18 June 2013, http://www.innovcity.fr/2013/06/18/nice-inaugure-

premier-boulevard-connecte-
du-monde/ (consulted 2
December 2014).
31 'Stratégie smart city du
Grand Lyon', http://www.
economie.grandlyon.com/
smart-city-strategie-politique-
lyon-ville-intelligente-durable-
france.347.0.html (consulted
10 December 2014).
32 https://nest.com/
thermostat/life-with-nest-
thermostat/ (consulted 18
January 2015).
33 Patrice Flichy, Le Sacre
de l'amateur: Sociologie des
passions ordinaires à l'ère
numérique, Le Seuil (Paris),
2010.
34 http://energy.gov/data/
green-button (consulted 18
January 2015).
35 PewResearch Internet
Project, 'Mobile Technology
Fact Sheet', http://www.
pewinternet.org/fact-sheets/
mobile-technology-fact-sheet/
(consulted 2 December 2014).
36 ComScore, 'Smartphones
Reach Majority in all EU5
Countries', 5 March 2013,
http://www.comscore.
com/Insights/Data-Mine/
Smartphones-Reach-Majority-
in-all-EU5-Countries (consulted
2 December 2014).

37 Warc, 'Smartphone
Ownership Surges in India', 28
February 2014, http://www.
warc.com/LatestNews/News/
EmailNews.news?ID=32643&
Origin=WARCNewsEmail&u
tm_source=WarcNews&utm_
medium=email&utm_
campaign=WarcNews20140228
(consulted 2 December 2014);
Charles Arthur, 'Smartphone
Explosion in 2014 Will See
Ownership in India Pass US',
The Guardian, 13 January
2014, http://www.theguardian.
com/technology/2014/jan/13/
smartphone-explosion-2014-
india-us-china-firefoxos-
android (consulted 2 December
2014).
38 Gilles Lipovetsky and Jean
Serroy, L'Ecran global: Du
Cinéma au smartphone [2007],
Le Seuil (Paris), 2011.
39 'Santander City
Brain', http://www.
santandercitybrain.com/
(consulted 18 January 2015).
40 This notion was for instance
at the core of the exhibition
'Toward the Sentient City'
curated by Mark Shepard in
the autumn of 2009 at the
Architectural League, New
York, http://www.sentientcity.
net/exhibit/ (consulted 2

December 2014); see also
Shepard (ed) 2001.
41 Antoine Picon, Ornament:
The Politics of Architecture and
Subjectivity, Wiley (Chichester),
2013. See also chapter 3.
42 See for instance Caroline
Jones (ed), Sensorium:
Embodied Experience,
Technology, and Contemporary
Art, MIT Press (Cambridge,
Massachusetts), 2006; and
François Ascher, Le Mangeur
hypermoderne, Odile Jacob
(Paris), 2005.
43 Mirko Zardini (ed), Sense
of the City: An Alternative
Approach to Urbanism,
Canadian Centre for
Architecture (Montreal) and
Lars Müller (Baden), 2005.
44 Michèle Leloup et al,
Pavillon France, Shanghai
Expo 2010, Jacques Ferrier
Architectures, Cofres Sas,
Archibooks (Paris), 2010.
45 Christine McLaren, 'The
Senseable City: An Interview
with Carlo Ratti', http://blogs.
guggenheim.org/lablog/the-
senseable-city-an-interview-
with-carlo-ratti/ (consulted 2
December 2014).
46 Richard Florida, The Rise
of the Creative Class: And
How It's Transforming Work,

*Leisure, Community, and Everyday Life*, Basic Books (New York), 2002.

**47** 'MIT's Kendall Square Initiative', http://web.mit.edu/newsoffice/kendall-square/ (consulted 2 December 2014).

**48** See Brett Goldstein and Lauren Dyson, *Beyond Transparency: Open Data and the Future of Civic Innovation*, Code for America (San Francisco), 2013.

**49** Jay Forrester, *Urban Dynamics*, MIT Press (Cambridge, Massachusetts), 1969.

**50** Colin Harrison and Ian Abbott Donnelly, 'A Theory of Smart Cities', *Proceedings of the 55th Annual Meeting of the International Society for the Systems Sciences* (Hull, UK), 2011, http://journals.isss.org/index.php/proceedings55th/article/viewFile/1703/572 (consulted 17 December 2014); Michael

Batty, *The New Science of Cities*, MIT Press (Cambridge, Massachusetts), 2013.

**51** See Gabriel Dupuy and Joel Tarr (eds), *Technology and the Rise of the Networked City in Europe and America*, Temple University Press (Philadelphia), 1988; and Olivier Coutard, Richard Hanley and Rae Zimmerman (eds), *Sustaining Urban Networks: The Social Diffusion of Large Technical Systems*, Routledge (London), 2004.

**52** Paul Virilio, *Ce qui arrive*, Actes Sud (Arles), 2002 (English version: *Unknown Quantity*, Thames & Hudson (London), 2003).

**53** Société d'Exploitation de la Tour Eiffel, Annual Report for 2013, http://www.tour-eiffel.biz/images/PDF/ra%202013.pdf (consulted 17 December 2014).

**54** On the strategic narratives meant to guide the

development of Paris and its region, see Pierre Veltz, *Paris, France, Monde: Repenser l'économie par le territoire*, Éditions de l'Aube (La Tour-d'Aigues), 2012.

**55** 'Un bit n'est ni une particule de matière, ni un élément d'idée, c'est un atome de circonstance': Pierre Lévy, *La Machine univers: Création, cognition et culture informatique*, La Découverte (Paris), 1987, p 124.

**56** On the SAGE system, see Paul Edwards, *The Closed World: Computers and the Politics of Discourse in Cold War America*, MIT Press (Cambridge, Massachusetts), 1996.

**57** Elodie Vieille Blanchard, 'Modelling the Future: An Overview of the "Limits to Growth" Debate', *Centaurus*, vol 52, 2010, pp 91–116.

# A Tale of Two Cities

## 2

Beyond the emphasis that is placed on occurrences, events and scenarios, the quest for the smart city has taken two separate paths that may appear contradictory at first glance. It is as though two distinct projects were emerging simultaneously in the name of a single ideal and within a single movement of city transformation through information and communications technology. The first identifies itself with the cybernetics of the 1950s and 1960s in its desire to anticipate and master everything. Seemingly in opposition to this neocybernetics-inspired smart city, with its deliberately technocratic emphasis, is the notion of a city that sets out to reinvest its citizens with the capacity spontaneously to invent community living, reviving the sense of festival whose disappearance from contemporary urban experience was lamented by the Situationists and indeed by the French sociologist Henri Lefebvre.[1]

Programmed monitoring of the way the city functions, largely based on more effective management of its essential infrastructure, from water and sanitation to transport; or a spontaneous, collaborative and festive urban experience that harnesses the resources of Web 2.0? Even though this opposition runs through most debates concerning the smart city, it needs to be placed in context. Its source is first and foremost in the fundamental ambivalence of the notion of the event, between a foreseeable occurrence and the unexpected arising of something new.[2] As an occurrence that falls within a predetermined range of possibilities, the event can indeed be largely anticipated. However, from the first malfunctioning of a complex technological system to a political revolution, it can also prove to be the bringer of change that could not have been foreseen and which renders obsolete the development scenarios that had been envisaged before it happened. While the neocybernetics-inspired city tends to favour the foreseeable dimension of events, the spontaneist and collaborative city counts on its capacity to periodically thwart calculations, models and simulations. But in fact these are two aspects of a single reality marked by the spread of digital culture, which magnifies the impact of what happens. Although information and communications technology takes on different forms depending on the viewpoint adopted – while the neocybernetics-inspired city tends to favour the development of integrated platforms, the collaborative city accords far greater importance to the use of mobile terminals, beginning with smartphones – both still rely on the same type of digital infrastructure based on sensors, chips, wireless transmission, information processing units and databases. Above all, both set out to mobilise individuals by making them inseparable from a technological universe that is supposed to be ever more closely adapted to their own characteristics. By the same token, the theme of the cyborg – that mixture of flesh and technology which was conceived in the Cold War period before being made popular by Hollywood cinema – can be found in both the city based on an ideal of foreseeability and the one that banks on its inhabitants' potential for spontaneous creation.

Although this chapter may appear to be a tale of two cities, both of them ought to be interpreted rather as avatars, in the original sense of incarnation, of a single urban reality that is currently emerging. These avatars prove themselves to be the carriers of two directions of development for city intelligence which, far from being mutually exclusive, are in fact mutually supportive. Nascent city intelligence needs to be imagined as a crossover between centralised control modules and a looser group of structures for exchange and deliberation that takes more after the network, or even the swarm.

# Neocybernetic Temptation

At the end of the previous chapter, I referred to the links between the intelligent city understood as a group of events, or event-city, and the world of video games. Besides the gamification of urban experience, there is another link between these two phenomena. It resides in the temptation to bring all the problems that face city administrators and decision-makers down to a question of management – a temptation whose origins can be found in the Cold War-era accumulation of research that is now designated by the generic term 'cybernetics'. The term was coined by the American mathematician and professor at MIT, Norbert Wiener, and he used it as a title for his 1948 book *Cybernetics, or Control and Communication in the Animal and the Machine*.[3]

Initially, cybernetics aimed to establish improved coupling between the human and an ever more complex technological environment, by considering both as information processing systems that obey a certain number of general principles, starting with the existence of feedback loops that allow them to regulate their behaviour. Wiener laid the foundations of this new and determinedly interdisciplinary field by focusing on problems of anti-aircraft defence during the Second World War.[4] Cybernetics remained branded by these military origins for a long time. At the height of the Cold War, it notably needed to allow fighters to adapt to ever more sophisticated weapons systems. The idea of a steering method based on a sort of fusion between humankind and machines was never far away. The term 'cybernetics' is furthermore derived from the Greek word *kubernetes*, meaning a ship's pilot.

The cybernetic approach is founded on a resolutely reductionist view of humankind and the world. According to the writings of the first cyberneticists, the brain is a machine with discrete states, very close to a computer. The central role accorded to information processing and self-regulation guarantees the possibility of a true symbiosis between humankind and machines. By the same token, cybernetics is partially related to research on the possibility of crossing

Cover of Edmund Callis Berkeley's *Giant Brains, or Machines that Can Think*, John Wiley & Sons (New York), 1949
The rise of cybernetics and the development of the computer were inseparable from the emergence of a reductionist attitude leading to an interpretation of life as information processing.

Joel Kinnaman in the title role in José Padilha's *RoboCop* remake, 2014
The hero of the RoboCop franchise, a severely wounded policeman who becomes a superhero thanks to a series of prostheses that transform him into an almost invincible warrior, is emblematic of the success met by the figure of the cyborg in Hollywood pop culture. Although he has been programmed by his creators to be obedient like a machine, RoboCop succeeds in maintaining a certain degree of freedom. His character symbolises the resistance of the human mind to the enslaving power of unbridled technology.

humans with machines through prosthetics, grafts and transplants, thus giving rise to cyborgs.[5] Half creatures of fantasy, half a research programme for Cold War military-industrial apparatus, cyborgs later came to be among the favourite characters of American science-fiction cinema: think for example of Ridley Scott's *Blade Runner* which was released in 1982, Paul Verhoeven's *RoboCop* which first came out in 1987 followed by two sequels in 1990 and 1993 and a remake in 2014, and the *Terminator* series which began in 1984 with the first film by James Cameron portraying the Connor family and terrifying machines that were hybrids of flesh, silicon and steel, charged with the task of exterminating them.[6]

In many ways, gamers on their computers or consoles are successors of the pilots of cybernetics. The blend of finely honed reflexes and swift processing of information are precisely one of the objectives of the cybernetic approach. During the development of cybernetics, at the borderline between academic research and military-industrial programmes, it sought to steer increasingly complex technological environments on the model of a system such as SAGE. While aeroplane cockpits may have initially appeared as the favoured form of habitat for the first cybernetic pilots – who took after cyborgs in their ability to internalise the machine's functioning logic, even if they did not yet possess artificial limbs – the control room and the operational control centre became the new locations for a humanity that was on the point of being hybridised with technology. The period from 1950 to 1970 was marked by a real fascination with these sorts of places.[7] Countless articles, documentaries and fictional films evoke derivatives of the NASA control room and of the NORAD command centre, both successors of the War Rooms from the Second World War which already manifested a vision of the world in terms of objectives to be reached and the data necessary to do so. The control room and command centre seem to be preludes to a universal immersion in a world where information is required to reign supreme, as in a new fluid environment in which humans and machines are steeped together. Although it has crystallised to some extent on the surface of those strange windows on the world that are video screens, its omnipresence appears to herald today's ubiquitous computing. Some aspects of computer games recall the world of the control room or command centre, with their multiple windows allowing different parameters to be managed in the manner of a general who coordinates his marching troops from the safety of an underground shelter decked out with columns of numbers, maps and diagrams.

The cybernetics of the 1950s and 1960s therefore appeared as a catch-all discipline. It tended to be allied to systems theory, sharing with it a reductionist vision of the world as well as notions of feedback loops and self-regulation. It later gave rise to the first research on artificial intelligence. In terms of fields of application, however, it expanded very rapidly indeed.

**The command centre of NORAD, Cheyenne Mountain, Colorado, c 2005**
Less dramatic than the movie set used in the 1983 film *WarGames*, the real NORAD command centre is nevertheless typical of a space in which the world is perceived through the lens of information, as an endless stream of events and scenarios that only cyborg-like creatures can fully master. The Cold War saw a multiplication of such spaces in parallel with research aiming at a more efficient coupling between humans, information systems and machines.

It was in this context, closely linked to systems theory, that a proliferation of attempts arose to apply its founding principles to cities.[8] New York, Los Angeles, Washington and many other American cities undertook experiments along these lines during the decades that followed the Second World War.[9] In order to do so, these cities' elected officials and technicians called upon consultancies that had proved themselves in planning large-scale military programmes such as the RAND Corporation, a think-tank that was originally funded by the US Air Force. If cities can be compared to complex organisms, or to a mixture of human organisation and technological infrastructure, why not envisage steering and orienting their development much as one might drive a tank, pilot an aeroplane or lead strategic equipment policies?

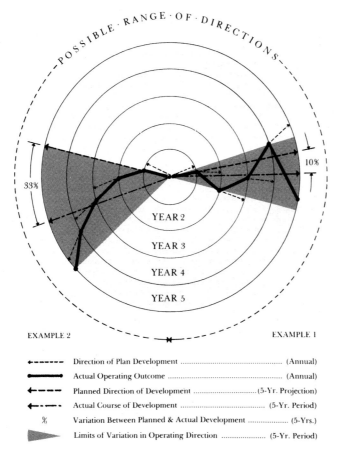

Melville Campbell Branch, conceptualised outcomes of continuous city planning, from *Continuous City Planning: Integrating Municipal Management and City Planning*, John Wiley & Sons (New York), 1981
The notion of 'continuous city planning' developed by Melville Branch owes much to the cybernetic ideal of efficient steering. The analogy between city planning and the task of a pilot is further reinforced by a presentation in which the resulting evolution of the city appears as a trajectory on a background reminiscent of a radar screen.

POSSIBLE · RANGE · OF · DIRECTIONS

33%

10%

YEAR 2
YEAR 3
YEAR 4
YEAR 5

EXAMPLE 2                                        EXAMPLE 1

- - - - - → Direction of Plan Development ............................................. (Annual)

━━━━━ Actual Operating Outcome ................................................... (Annual)

← - - - Planned Direction of Development ..........................(5-Yr. Projection)

← - ·— · Actual Course of Development ..................................... (5-Yr. Period)

% Variation Between Planned & Actual Development .................. (5-Yrs.)

Limits of Variation in Operating Direction ................... (5-Yr. Period)

And then why not likewise envisage an urban control room, along the lines of military command posts, where information necessary to the management of the city would be displayed? After a detour in armaments project management for the Ramo-Wooldridge Corporation, a company notably responsible for developing missile programmes, the American urbanist Melville Branch made a breakthrough in the early 1960s when he proposed a centre for urban planning of this type for the city of Los Angeles.[10] Some ten years later, Salvador Allende's Chile went even further by conceiving, under the direction of the British cyberneticist Stafford Beer, a computerised control and planning room for the Chilean economy. After the big city, an entire nation. In contrast to Branch's urban planning centre, the Chilean project, dubbed Cybersyn, was almost brought to completion, although the 1973 coup d'état cut short the experiment.[11]

Branch's centre and the Cybersyn control room needed to allow a visualisation of events and situations rather than things, as in an operational

Melville Campbell Branch, city planning centre for Los Angeles, from *Continuous City Planning: Integrating Municipal Management and City Planning*, John Wiley & Sons (New York), 1981
Imagined in the 1960s for Los Angeles, Branch's city planning centre owes much to military control rooms or operations centres. In this enclosed space, the city appears as an information-driven system.

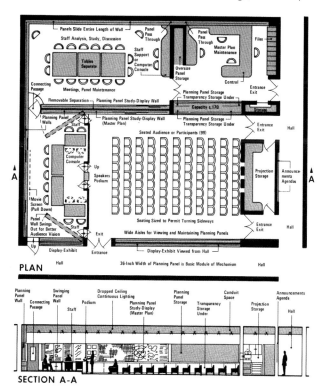

control centre. This type of proposal could appear obsolete a priori, given the extent to which it seems to replicate the original War Rooms model. Even so, it has become topical again over the last few years. Indeed, proposals inspired by entirely comparable sources have reappeared in the context of some smart city development projects.

'Not far from Copacabana Beach, here is a control room that looks straight out of NASA.'[12] Thus begins an article in the *New York Times* on the new Operations Center designed by IBM for the city of Rio de Janeiro. Revealingly, the initial impetus behind the creation of this centre by IBM's Smarter Cities division came from an event: a natural disaster, a storm that had caused flooding and major landslides in 2010 and had served to reveal an absence of coordination structure among the emergency services. The employees within the Operations Center face a wall of screens – 'a sort of virtual Rio, rendered in real time', as the journalist describes it. The Center runs a sophisticated weather forecasting program that allows rainfall in the various districts of the city to be predicted. It receives video images from the main public areas and

Project Cybersyn, general view of the Operations Room, Santiago de Chile, 1973
This futuristic space designed to manage the Chilean economy featured white fibreglass swivel chairs, somewhat reminiscent of science-fiction spaceship seats, and a series of screens displaying crucial information on the state of the country. The room was destroyed in 1973 after the coup d'état that overthrew the government of Salvador Allende.

metro stations. A map displays car accidents, power cuts, in short everything that happens which could disrupt public order.

One of the innovations in comparison to the Cold War control rooms lies in the extent of real-time video coverage. In the coming years, this is likely to go even further. It is conceivable that intervention teams will be equipped with video cameras, on the model of what happens in the armed forces. The army general holed up in his underground command post can follow his troops' progress as well as the obstacles that they encounter on the ground, thanks to the video capture equipment that more and more of them are carrying. The Iraq War and more recently the capture of Osama bin Laden in Pakistan have made us accustomed to this constant to-ing and fro-ing between general information and subjective video cameras. Rio de Janeiro has not gone that far yet, but events are displayed there simultaneously in statistical form, as flashing dots on maps, and in video.

**IBM Rio de Janeiro Operations Center, 2010**
Rio Operations Center appears as the distant successor of Cold War control rooms. On the screens, what happens in the city is displayed in order to trigger the appropriate response. The entire facility seems to be conceived as an instrument of rational steering in the purest cybernetic vein.

For IBM and its rivals – such as Cisco Systems, which has played a major role in the construction of Songdo – the realisation of this type of project has a symbolic character. Even if the range of solutions proposed by these firms goes far beyond these centralised projects, the latter have the merit of showing in the most spectacular way possible that 'smart city' applications can allow cities to be steered more efficiently. The neocybernetic inspiration of these control rooms that are intended to concentrate, coordinate and process the copious amounts of information provided by the sensors and video cameras of the smart city is not unlike the world of computer gaming – *SimCity* in particular – where the gamer must not only build the city but also protect it from disasters ranging from flooding to invasion by aliens. A similar relationship is evident in the approach of companies such as Simudyne, which specialises in creating simulations for businesses and is currently eyeing up the urban realm. As the firm's website notably says: 'We build places where decisions can be made, tested, and understood. We call them decision spaces: created worlds engineered to match the real [...] – what works in the real world, works in our decision spaces.'[13] The same ideal of rational management permeates both the control room and computer simulation. It also

**Screenshot from the Maxis video game *SimCity Social*, 2012**
The different versions of *SimCity* all rely on a neocybernetic urban vision in which players have to adjust key parameters correctly in order to ensure the harmonious growth of their city.

inspires projects that are oriented more towards mass data collection, such as the smart city section of the new Hudson Yards district of New York, developed in collaboration with New York University's Center for Urban Science and Progress. The latter sets out to contribute to a better understanding of the way in which cities function, through gathering information in buildings and from users via sensors and smartphone apps.[14] Big data and neocybernetic temptation are happy bedfellows.

It would be easy at this stage to go on at length about the seductiveness of this type of approach, and of course about its limitations. In Rio de Janeiro, the initiative came from the city's mayor, Eduardo Paes. The attraction of this type of tool for elected officials and municipal technicians, as they seek to increase their efficiency by concentrating information and exploring different development scenarios, is obvious. It can be supposed that such a prospect is not without interest for promoters of initiatives such as the 'connected boulevard' in Nice or the smart city area of the Hudson Yards district.

As for the limitations, these can be summed up in a paraphrase of the American architect Christopher Alexander's famous phrase 'a city is not a tree', meaning a logic tree, by noting that the city is not a system either.[15] When it reigns unchallenged, neocybernetic temptation is founded on an exaggeratedly simplified approach to the city: an approach whose operational character may well prove disappointing, beyond the maintenance of basic infrastructure and the coordination of intervention on the ground such as that of the police and fire brigade. Moreover, this is what the Rio Operations Center mainly does, and with varying success depending on the circumstances – as witness the flaws that appeared during the organisation of World Youth Day in 2013, from the Pope's being caught up in a traffic jam upon his arrival to the disruptions and changes of programme caused by heavy rain. We are still a long way from Melville Branch-style generalised monitoring and planning.

The city is not a system, or at least it is not one of those systems that involve the finite numbers of parameters and feedback loops of which modellers are so fond. Although neocybernetic temptation goes hand in hand with the reactivation of urban modelling practices that were in full swing between 1950 and 1970 (as discussed in the previous chapter), it would seem unlikely for these practices to lead to integrated city management. This does not mean that there is nothing to gain by trying to better monitor and predict certain aspects of city functioning. On the contrary: despite its limitations, neocybernetic temptation constitutes one of the elements of the smart city, and one that is probably necessary in areas such as monitoring networks, maintaining order and the fight against natural disasters. It also has much to contribute when combined with practices of data mining that can reveal hitherto neglected dimensions of urban functioning. We simply need to beware of overly extreme attempts at integration, which would end up compromising the viability of operations of monitoring and intervention. Above all, we need to make sure that this inclination does not stifle other directions of development.

## The Cyborg-City Hypothesis

But let us suspend the discussion on the advantages and disadvantages of this type of prospect, and look instead at what its implications are in terms of the meaning that can be given to the expression 'smart city'. A first hypothesis, abundantly conjured up in science fiction, lies in the progressive setting up of an artificial intelligence such as La or HAL (as mentioned in the previous chapter). Such a scenario is admittedly, however, far from winning the votes of those involved in research and development on the theme of the smart city, for reasons related to both feasibility and the potentially dangerous character of such a development.

Regarding feasibility, we are still a long way from the 'technological singularity' promised by the American engineer Ray Kurzweil: the moment when the intelligence of machines overtakes that of humankind.[16] Above all, even supposing that such a moment is coming, they would still need to reach a level of understanding and control of urban organisms that are even more complex than the human brain. It cannot be assumed that machines, even highly developed ones, could be capable of understanding cities so much better than the people who created them. As for the desirability or otherwise of this type of development, films and novels have repeatedly warned us against the risks of a digital Big Brother whose objectives could differ widely from our own. This divergence between human interests and the interests of intelligent machines was already one of the themes of *2001: A Space Odyssey*; and *Terminator* and *The Matrix* have since completed the demonstration. In a BBC interview, the British astrophysicist Stephen Hawking has gone even further than these already very pessimistic scenarios by affirming that 'the development of full artificial intelligence could spell the end of the human race'.[17]

Behind these apocalyptic visions, it is possible to imagine limited forms of artificial intelligence charged with partial management missions, without the future of humanity being compromised. After all, a whole range of urban infrastructure already functions in an automated fashion. In this case, instead of the much-feared scenario of a digital Big Brother, we would find ourselves in the presence of a group of less developed forms of intelligence, with limited remits and supervised by human operators. These forms of intelligence would however be capable of dialoguing with their operators as well as with each other. The model of the all-powerful solitary machine would thus be substituted by a more conversational approach. We will return to this idea of conversation later on. We are more likely to see the smart city emerging through interactions between human stakeholders and programs invested with certain functions of reasoning, than as the result of centralised processes.

In the meantime, in line with the heritage of cybernetics, it would seem appropriate to visualise another track – that of the cyborg – in order to sketch out what the smart city could mean in concrete terms within the perspective of the neocybernetic-type management of what happens. Because, leaving aside the recourse to entirely artificial intelligence, we are driven to envisage a coupling between human stakeholders and city infrastructure, which relies on ever more sophisticated digital tools. In this case, the smart city would be a cyborg-city. We have yet to understand how such a coupling, or rather hybridisation, might come about, and above all to ask questions on the extent and organisation of its human component.

The idea of resorting to the theme of cyborgs in order to analyse the contemporary urban condition has inspired a number of authors over the last fifteen years or so. In an essay entitled 'La Ville territoire des cyborgs' ('The City as Cyborg Territory'), I suggested in 1998 that the cyborg could represent for the city of today – a city that is both ever more spread out and suffused by digital networks – the equivalent of what the figure of the ideal man represented for the Renaissance city: a fiction allowing a better understanding of some aspects of the logic that makes up the urban environment, together with the profound nature of individual experience that is supposed to correspond to it.[18] While Renaissance man reflected a productive exchange between a new form of subjectivity and the construction of an objective world order founded on mathematics and perspective, the cyborg expressed the individual's greater dependence on technology in the digital era. The MIT professor William J Mitchell also summoned up the cyborg in a 2003 book, *Me++: The Cyborg Self and the Networked City*, because of its capacity to express the ever-increasing inseparability of humankind and technology.[19] With regard to our subject, Mitchell's book – which found inspiration in the writings of the British–American anthropologist and cyberneticist Gregory Bateson, and particularly in his 1972 collection of essays *Steps to an Ecology of Mind* – particularly insisted on the necessity of getting past a vision of individuals as self-contained, and considering them instead as complex environments, or indeed ecologies, displaying themselves in successive layers formed of atoms, data bits and electromagnetic waves, from their bodies to the wireless networks that allow them to be connected, via their clothing and the walls of their homes.[20]

While this type of approach was centred on the individual, the UK-based geographers Matthew Gandy and especially Erik Swyngedouw were beginning a transition towards the application of the cyborg theme to urban infrastructure.[21] Swyngedouw was particularly headed in that direction, as he introduced the notion of metabolism in order to account for the new operating mode of the contemporary city, both biological and technological.

The notion of metabolism is all the more interesting since it allows a realisation of the intensification of the sanitary or even genetic dimension of the coupling between humankind and urban infrastructure, in line with the advent of this 'biopolitical' era heralded by the French philosopher Michel Foucault around the mid-1970s.[22] A new stage in this direction was reached when the authorities in Singapore imposed a requirement on whole sectors of their population, notably including schoolchildren and soldiers, to measure their body temperature daily during the freak pneumonia epidemic of 2003.[23] Taking things even further, a team of researchers from MIT's SENSEable City Lab has devised a system of continuous monitoring of sewerage that relies on statistical analysis of people's microbiota – the ensemble of bacteria, fungus and other micro-organisms that live in symbiosis with humans – which would require regular sampling from cities' waste water systems.[24] Besides this type of project, the startup company MC10, in partnership with Ericsson, is developing a sensing sticker, Biostamp, that can collect and transmit data such as body temperature, heart rate, brain activity and exposure to ultraviolet radiation.[25] Similar projects are being pursued all around the world, from Japan to Switzerland.

At the crossroads of traditional surveillance and monitoring techniques and new tools for screening and diagnostics that are being hurriedly launched, from biometry to DNA sequencing, it is possible to imagine an ever more

intimate coupling between the city and its inhabitants. The notion of urban metabolism becomes more relevant day by day. The hypothesis of the cyborg-city recalls this vision that is on the verge of becoming reality.

The fact remains that the notion of the cyborg has long applied to the individual and that, in the hybridisation of human and machine, it is generally the human component that is supposed to perform the functions related to consciousness and decision-making.[26] This primacy allowed the American anthropologist Donna Haraway to dramatically invert the interpretation of the cyborg in her 'A Cyborg Manifesto' of 1985, which has become a social sciences classic.[27] Instead of seeing the cyborg as a creature produced and dominated by military-industrial apparatus, Haraway made it the hero of a possible liberation linked to its hybrid nature, which crosses common boundaries and is thus indifferent to questions of gender and class.

University of Tokyo professor Takao Someya displays the world's lightest and thinnest flexible integrated circuits and touch sensor system at a press conference in Tokyo on 24 July 2014 Much thinner than Biostamp, this flexible electrical circuit weighing less than a feather could enable the implantation of sensors inside the body. The device can be used to monitor all sorts of physical data, such as body temperature and blood pressure as well as electronic pulses from muscles or the heart.

In the cyborg-city, every individual must be considered as a cyborg. This city must also be imagined as a collection of hybrids formed on different scales by the association of human groups and technical devices. The latter make it possible to speak of cyborg infrastructure, networks and communities. The properties of the cyborg are transmitted from the individual to the community, and from elementary infrastructure to complex networks. Such an interweaving of hybrid entities recalls Gottfried Leibniz's definition of organic life as a machine whose tiniest cogs are themselves machines which in turn harbour other machines.[28] But while it evokes the seductive characterisation of life proposed by Leibniz, this cascade of hybridisation between human and technology cannot entirely resolve the question of how to manage the cyborg-city, which is inevitably a political question since it leads us to ask who is directing it, and by what means?

It is tempting to return to a conversational model, considering the urban population as the pilot, or rather as a group of pilots each responsible for a particular field and interacting with each other along the lines of a conversation. But this view does not truly resolve the issue of good government. How can decisions be taken which go beyond mere co-ordination and optimisation and that do not adversely affect any of the parties involved? In our current state of awareness, we need to accept to rely either on politics as we know it, or on a set of algorithms that allow a synthesis of the needs and wishes of every individual; that is, thousands or indeed millions of intentions and plans concerning the management of the city and the directions that its development might take.

When neocybernetic temptation and the hypothesis of the cyborg-city are pushed to their extremes, the balance tips towards the second option, and all the more so since the limitations of traditional democracy are being measured every day in the face of Web 2.0. As the French telecommunications sociologist Dominique Cardon notes, the Internet itself is not administered through democratic means, and people rarely end up voting in online debates.[29] But short of returning completely to automatic procedures of integration and optimisation, which would link back to the idea of a digital Big Brother, we need in reality to imagine a mixed solution where the play of algorithms is tempered by human organisation that is capable of correcting its excesses. Somewhere at the core of this organisation, which would constitute a true urban government, there would need to be a body of experts responsible for determining the parameters to be taken into account in managing the city, as well as the procedures and rules regulating the production of information and the optimisation of needs and wishes, and of intentions and plans. Such experts would be the city's true pilots.

In these conditions, it is hard to see how it might be possible to avoid the pitfall of a technocracy being constituted, upstream from politics, which would formulate the rules of a new type of game: a serious game par excellence, consisting of managing the city in the manner of a vast system. Experts from both academia and business already form a substantial presence in organisations such as the Smart London Board, created by the mayor Boris Johnson in 2013, which has generated a *Smart London Plan* intended to draw up the British capital's strategy in terms of applying digital technology to the city.[30] Of course, such experts' powers of decision-making currently remain limited, and politicians reaffirm loud and clear that the citizen is at the heart of their approach. But will this always be the case in future? If they are given free rein, neocybernetic temptation and the hypothesis of the cyborg-city will lead to a technocratic management of the urban realm, or even to a reduction of politics to sound administration of not just things, as the French political and economic theorist Henri de Saint-Simon and his followers suggested at the dawn of the 19th century, but also events: of what happens.[31]

## Spontaneous City, Collaborative City

Technology rarely constitutes an inevitable factor that weighs down on the course of history in the way that natural constraints do. To be convinced of this, we need only bear in mind the fact that the mobilisation of vast hydraulic resources does not necessarily lead to the type of oriental despotism that the German-American historian Karl August Wittfogel associated with it when he applied the examples of Ancient Mesopotamia and Egypt on a general level.[32] The case of Holland, with its dams, dykes and polders, speaks out against this type of generalisation. In reality, technology displays a significant degree of social and political indeterminacy. In the case of the smart city, this indeterminacy is expressed through the existence of another model than that of the technocratically managed cyborg-city. In contrast to

Flash mob dancing at Sergels Torg for Gay Pride, Stockholm, 3 August 2012
Flash mobs are emblematic of another type of smart city in which digital technology would serve as a platform enabling urban spontaneity.

Opposition supporters talk near graffiti referring to the social networking site Twitter in Tahrir Square in Cairo, 5 February 2011
A photograph that conveys the role played by social media in recent political and social uprisings such as the Arab Spring.

neocybernetic temptation are the desires and experiences of spontaneity and collaboration that are just as present in the contemporary urban landscape.

Even if they are prepared in advance, the success encountered by smart mobs – sudden gatherings in public spaces that are made possible by the mobilisation of participants through social networks and mobile phones – bears witness to a desire for spontaneous expression that cannot be satisfied within the usual frameworks of public speaking and collective action.[33] The latter seems related to the festive ambitions of the Situationists and Henri Lefebvre. And what if the right to the city were also, fundamentally, a right to collective demonstration and celebration? In opposition to the city that is programmed like a well-oiled machine stands the city that gives priority back to the creative mobilisation of its citizens.

With smart mobs and their more artistically inclined counterparts, flash mobs, we may well ask ourselves whether the preparation of the event falls more into the realm of programming rather than being rooted in authentic spontaneity. However, the role played by the social networks, led by Twitter, in a whole series of political and social movements, notably in the uprisings of the Arab Spring between 2010 and 2014, incites us to get over this sort of objection.[34] These examples demonstrate that the digital realm can serve as a basis for real events, in the fullest sense of the term. The close association between mobilisation through information and communications technology and occupation of public spaces that suddenly regain a political character, from Tahrir Square in Cairo to Taksim Square in Istanbul, equally provides food for thought. Here again, nothing forces us to perceive the links between the electronic world and physical space along the lines of the top-down model of neocybernetic management of urban facilities and metabolism.

The desire for collaboration may well be even more significant than aspirations for rediscovered spontaneity. One of its favoured forms of expression is in the extraordinary flourishing of participative and collaborative businesses that has been made possible by the advent of Web 2.0 and which forms another access route to the smart city. Some of these businesses have taken on a global dimension, such as OpenStreetMap, a free mapping database that relies on voluntary participation for its development and which was approaching the two-million-user mark at the beginning of 2015.[35] This has been emulated by others all around the world, such as FixMyStreet, a website on which UK citizens can indicate damage to public space near their homes, from potholes in roads and pavements to blocked drains.[36] Local versions of FixMyStreet also exist in Australia, Canada, Korea, Greece, Japan,

**People gathered on Tahrir Square in Cairo on 9 February 2011, to demand the resignation of President Mubarak**
Hundreds of thousands of people gathered on Tahrir Square at the climax of the Egyptian Revolution against President Hosni Mubarak. Throughout the events, the occupation of public space went along with the intensive use of digital media.

Sweden, Switzerland and Tunisia, without even mentioning all the other sites that are based on a similar idea. For their part, websites such as Waze allow drivers to help each other by sharing information on traffic and road conditions in real time.[37]

While cities are all abuzz with exchanges on such sites, the practice of crowdfunding has developed for both private and public projects. In particular there has been an increase in the number of educational and participatory spaces, such as the fabrication laboratories or 'fab labs' initially promoted by MIT's Center for Bits and Atoms, where people can learn the basics of digital fabrication, share files and know-how, and test new and original modes of cooperation.[38] These exchanges and practices contribute to the documentation and enrichment of the urban experience day by day. In contrast to the models inspired by cybernetics are those that produce a smart city founded in the fertile ground of discussions between individuals, which tend to be self-regulatory, on the model of the great wiki websites. In Rio de Janeiro, the top-down logic that is at work through the Operations Center finds its counterpart in the bottom-up approach that underpins initiatives such as Meu Rio (My Rio). This website allows the city's inhabitants to join

Eric Fischer, OpenStreetMap GPS trace density in and near Europe, April 2012
The picture shows the density of geographical information regarding Europe that had been posted on OpenStreetMap in April 2012. Countries such as Germany and the United Kingdom appear as especially active.

OpenStreetMap mapping
party in Milton Keynes,
16–17 May 2009
The document shows the
traces left by the various
contributors to the mapping
party. Each one of them was
equipped with a GPS receiver
with recording capability.
The aim of the party was
to add in the road network
of the town, as well as a
number of points of interest
such as pubs and major retail
buildings.

- Thewinch - Area 6+8 - combo
- Jvvw - Area 19 - 20090516
- Firefishy - Area 38+39 - 20090516
- Kepa - Area 8 - 20090516
- Ojw - Area 2+39 - combo
- Chris Parker - Area 3 - 2009-05-17
- Steve8 - Area 40+47 - combo

- Ed Loach - Area 45+46 - combo
- JBrown - Area 5 - 385704
- smsm1 - NCR6 - 388247
- smsm1 - Area 49 - 386852
- FixieDan - Area 26 - 385523
- TomS - Area 6+27+33+44 - combo
- Ollie - Area 22+23+NCR6 - combo

- Simonthomas - Area 7+50 - 385680
- AChadwick - Area 42+43 - clean combo
- Harry Wood - Area 0+24 - combo
- TomH - Area 29 - combo
- Jaszmania - Area 31+32 - combo
- Twain - Area 21+25+30
- Blackadder - Area 14+15 - combo

forces to fight for causes that are dear to them, from opposing eviction from
their homes to saving a local school.[39]

The outline of this spontaneous and collaborative smart city may remain far
more blurred than that of the neocybernetics-inspired smart city of which it
is the counterpart; but it nevertheless constitutes an alternative which should
be viewed as seriously as its rival. Businesses as powerful as IBM and Cisco
are not mistaken on this front, and they are developing platforms intended to
support more collaborative approaches to the urban realm, even if the degree
of collaboration that they envisage remains limited.

Like its rival, the spontaneous and participatory city possesses grey
areas. Firstly, most of its manifestations presuppose a certain degree of

Screenshot of the FixMyStreet United Kingdom website
Websites of this type have now become common in all major cities around the world. In Paris, an application called DansMaRue ('in my street') runs for instance on the Web as well as on smartphones.

centralised control, even if only to fix general frameworks and protocols of collaboration. Townsend's 'civic hackers' (discussed in the previous chapter) often play this role, with the ever-present risk that their power may one day be reinforced to the point of constituting a form of government that is more authoritarian than it may appear.[40] This is a question that is already being asked about networks such as Facebook, over which Mark Zuckerberg and his teams reign almost unchallenged; and the same question is being asked of businesses such as MindMixer which offer communities, schools and town councils the tools that allow them to gather opinions and promote public debate.[41] Secondly, on most collaborative websites, the number of contributors remains low in comparison to that of users, being for instance in the region of 1 per cent on OpenStreetMap.[42] More awkwardly, participation is very unevenly distributed, with a core

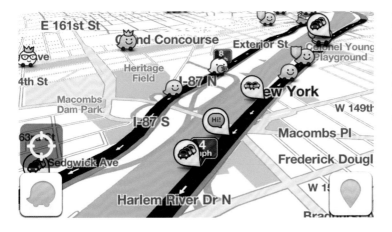

Screenshot of the Waze website, 2014
Members of the Waze community or 'Wazers', can alert other users of the application to speed traps, accidents, traffic jams, and even the best petrol prices by placing notifications over a simple, community-edited map.

Interior of FabLab
Lucerne, Switzerland, 2015
'Fab labs' like this one,
located in a loft space on
the campus of the Lucerne
University of Applied
Sciences and Arts, offer
the possibility to make
use of equipment such as
3D printers, laser cutters
and milling machines, to
turn ideas into reality. One
of the ambitions of this
type of place is also to
foster exchanges between
users, thus promoting a
collaborative vision of work
and leisure.

of highly motivated and productive contributors and a mass of occasional
contributors who are far less committed from day to day.

Nor should large-scale collaborative websites be imagined to call only upon
individuals. Many of them rely equally on the extensive use of automatic
software programs, or bots, which carry out tasks from correcting spelling
errors to monitoring the quality of contributions. Such is the case, for
example, with Wikipedia, which appears in many ways to be the most
accomplished model of participatory enterprise, as much for its number of
faithful volunteers around the world – nearly 24 million contributors being
registered at the beginning of 2015 – as for the quality of its results.[43] A series
of enlightening articles on this question by the American communication
specialists R Stuart Geiger, David Ribes, Aaron Halfaker and John Riedl
describe a three-tier structure for the revision of contributions, with bots at
the base, then cyborg-type assemblages between humans and computer
programs, and finally a higher level where humans reign supreme.[44]

This example encourages us not to think of the two cities discussed in this chapter as being mutually exclusive. Automatic computer programs and cyborg-type assemblages are found on both sides. Moreover, these cities reveal themselves to be complementary rather than in opposition to each other. There are some fields, albeit limited in number, where a neocybernetic type of management seems preferable to citizen engagement: think, for example, of the running of certain large-scale integrated automatic systems such as underground railway networks. In most cases, it is still better to rely on the capacity of individuals for self-organisation and cooperation, even if their contributions are moderated by the use of tools like those offered by firms such as MindMixer.

If the contrast is still current between the city that is regulated and managed from above and that which is supposed to be born of more or less spontaneous coordination in the manner of a giant wiki or mashup, it is because it harks back to another more fundamental question concerning the men and women of today and how they view their identity and its evolution. As the American urban sociologist Robert Park remarked some time ago, 'the city and the urban environment represent man's most consistent and, on the whole, his most successful attempt to remake the world he lives in more after his heart's desire'; and he added, aptly: 'In making the city, man has remade itself.'[45] But this undertaking rarely proves simple, even if only because desires are hardly ever unequivocal. The question of the individual is at the core of the smart city's contradictions, like the figure of the cyborg in which it is possible to see by turns a symbol of enslavement to the great commercial, industrial and military machine and of the possibility of radical liberation from the constraints that these systems bring to bear on us. What kind of smart city are we seeking to build?

Photomontage with activists affiliated to Meu Rio carrying signs that read 'Quem Não Vota Pela Educação Não Merece O Meu Voto' – those who don't vote for education do not deserve my vote Education for everyone is among the causes defended by Meu Rio. Since its launch in 2011, Meu Rio has successfully mobilised an online community to promote goals ranging from the fight against corruption to environmental protection.

What direction should it be taken in, if it is to be made sustainable? These questions amount to the same thing as asking ourselves what has become of us in the digital era, at the moment of its arrival and not necessarily only because of it: again, we need to avoid the trap of technological determinism. Above all we need to ask ourselves what we want to become in the future, without hiding our indecision and ambiguity.

## The Digital Individual

I repeat: the smart city accords very particular importance to individuals. First of all, through biometric techniques, digital technology allows for individuals to be precisely identified, and thus aids in the fight against threats ranging from identity theft to terrorism. With geolocation, to which we will return shortly, it is possible to know the position of mobile phone holders at any given moment, through triangulation between masts. In Singapore, London and Stockholm, it is cars that are the targets of individualised pinpointing, within the scope of tolls and congestion charges. Finally, information and communications technology, interacting with a whole set of methods of detection and surveillance, allows tracking of people's activities both in physical space and online.

Digital technology is linked to contemporary society's shift towards individualism, as noted by a large number of sociologists over the last twenty years or so.[46] Nicholas Negroponte, the founder of the Media Lab at MIT, made it one of the themes of his 1995 bestseller *Being Digital*.[47] At the heart of the increasing personalisation of content that Web 2.0 implies, the individual also plays a central role in the strengthening of key dimensions of urban experience such as the new importance of sensory determination. The sensory city is particularly aimed at individuals, even if only because they need to be persuaded to consume. Educated and talented individuals are supposed to be the driving force of the knowledge economy. More than anything else, they influence the possibility of sustainable urban development, which requires commitment from individuals who need to internalise the values and the codes of conduct on which practices such as the selective sorting of household waste rely.

Geared to the tensions that run through the ideal of the smart city as well as the process that leads to it, individuals of the digital era themselves appear to be contradictory. The figure of the cyborg allows a better

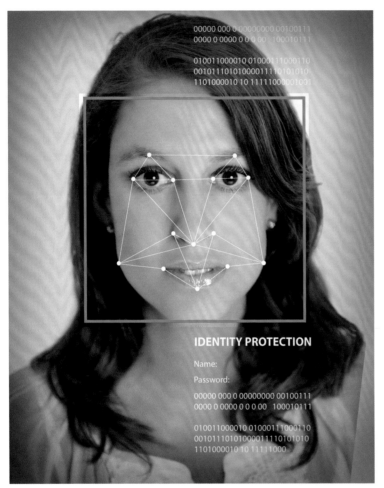

**IDENTITY PROTECTION**

Name:
Password:

00000 000 0 00000000 00100111
0000 0 0000 0 0 0 00  100010111

010011000010 01000111000110
0010111010100001111 10101010
1101000010 10 11111000

**Female face with lines from a facial recognition software program**
From fingerprints and retinal scanning to facial recognition, individual identification for security purposes represents a thriving business for all sorts of hardware and software companies.

understanding of some of these contradictions, beginning with the one that is emerging between growing submission to the diktats of the industrial and, most of all, the commercial machine – since the end of the Cold War, the military sphere has faded into the background – and the conviction that it is possible to escape their grasp. Amazon, Apple, eBay, Facebook, Google and Twitter impose their logics on hundreds of millions of clients, but these same clients cannot shake off the sense that they are simultaneously being allowed to develop their personalities. Social networks have proved typical of this situation, which is paradoxical at the very least. Almost all Facebook

**Security camera detects the movement of traffic on the rooftop of a skyscraper**
Surveillance cameras have become as common in cities as traffic lights. They monitor individuals as well as all sorts of other phenomena such as automobile traffic.

users are alarmed from time to time at the threats posed to their private life by Mark Zuckerberg's company's rules of confidentiality; but, for many members of the network, it is through updating their personal page that this private life is constructed.

Another contradiction that is inseparable from the previous one is the contrast between profound dependence on technology and the ambition to dominate it in order to fully become the masters of our destiny. On the one hand, the cyborg cannot exist without technological support at all times; on the other, it claims not to be a prisoner of it. This tension had appeared even before the advent of the cyborg theme and the development of digital technology. In fact, it is almost as old as the techniques of the industrial era, which are still on the verge of enslaving humankind while simultaneously retaining a quality of emancipation. From the first decades of the 19th century, the factory already appeared as a place of radical alienation at the same time as being a chance for whole sectors of the population, and particularly for young women, to break free from the dominance of their traditional family ties, thanks to salaried work. The Saint-Simonian economist

Michel Chevalier noted this duality when he visited the factories of the city of Lowell in Massachusetts in the early 1830s.[48] While Karl Marx's factory, as analysed in *Capital* (1867), chained the proletariat to the machine, Michel Chevalier's allowed female workers to liberate themselves from the stranglehold of their fathers, brothers and husbands.[49]

Digital technology lends a new flavour to this mixture of alienation and emancipation. It makes alienation more insidious, and fully compatible with the neoliberalism-inspired 'empire' that is the United States, the homeland of most of the great Internet businesses.[50] But it also seems to offer the promise at last of an ability to freely choose one's destiny, thanks to the multiplier effect of Web 2.0 which is supposed to allow individuals to make themselves heard without necessarily being subjected to the usual filters of institutions, recognised professional competence and social status. While the ultimate imperative of modernity consists in being oneself, as the French sociologist François de Singly affirms, it must be acknowledged that the 'consecration of the amateur' described by another French sociologist, Patrice Flichy, gives a new impulse to this project.[51]

**Police surveillance in Monterrey, Mexico, 18 December 2014**
Surveillance cameras are monitored by members of the Fuerza Civil (Civil Force) police unit during a media presentation at the police academy in Monterrey, in order to show the police model that the Mexican federal government wants to promote across the entire country.

The tensions and contradictions that are revealed by the coming together of digital technology and the individualist orientation of society today cannot be entirely reduced to the theme of the cyborg. Other approaches also need to be called into play, which place more emphasis on the intrinsic multiplicity of individuals than on the prospect of their being hybridised with machines. These approaches involve tensions of a quite different nature than the ones that are generated by the increasing intimacy between humans and technology.

Contemporary neuroscience has gradually accustomed us to no longer considering the brain as a centralised information processing unit, or a sort of giant calculator that conforms to the cybernetic representation of intelligence. Cerebral activity, including self-consciousness, appears instead to originate in a complex set of interactions within networks whose organisation and functioning is irresistibly reminiscent of the Internet. In a novel portraying a psychiatrist named Weber, the American writer Richard Powers perfectly summarises the content of this seductive analogy. 'He knew the drill,' writes Powers

**Cover of the *Lowell Offering*, January 1845**
A monthly periodical, the *Lowell Offering* published works of poetry and fiction by the young female workers of the Lowell, Massachusetts, textile mills of the early American industrial revolution. Modern industry did not only enslave workers. It offered possibilities of emancipation to some of them, including to the Lowell 'factory girls'.

of his protagonist; 'throughout history, the brain had been compared to the highest prevailing level of technology: steam engine, telephone switchboard, computer. Now, as Weber approached his own professional zenith, the brain became the Internet, a distributed network, more than two hundred modules in loose, mutually modifying chatter with other modules.'[52] The same type of interpretation could be applied to the functioning of the body as a whole.

Added to this fundamental biological diversity is the diversity of our lives as divided out across various networks – family, professional, friendship – which seem to correspond to different identities. Never quite the same from one context to another, we reveal ourselves to be very different from the

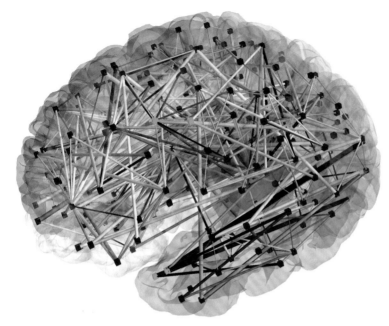

Stephan Gerhard, Patric Hagmann, Jean-Philippe Thiran, Connectome Mapping Toolkit, Ecole Polytechnique Fédérale de Lausanne and Université de Lausanne, Switzerland, 2010
A connectome is a comprehensive map of the neural connections in the brain. In Lausanne, a team has been working on an open-source framework to analyse and visualise connectomes. At this fundamental level, the contemporary subject appears as inherently multiple, network- or environment-like.

heroic figure to which we have so long tried to reduce individuality. Another way of expressing this diversity consists in considering the individual as an environment, or even an ecology, following the formula proposed by Gregory Bateson, who tried to reconcile the heritage of cybernetics with his culture as an anthropologist conscious of the difficulty of isolating humans from their milieu, which is inextricably both natural and cultural.[53] For a whole section of contemporary philosophy, from Gilles Deleuze to Bruno Latour and Peter Sloterdijk, such impossibility is a recurrent theme of reflection.[54] We are multiple and diverse in the sense that it is impossible for us to abstract ourselves from our environment and to consider ourselves as separate. Furthermore, many of the arguments for the necessity of sustainable development are based on the impossibility of abstracting ourselves from this environment. Our multiplicity and diversity also correspond to the many channels that unite us with our surroundings.

By helping to multiply our identities even further, digital technology makes this absence of separation more tangible. As the American sociologist Sherry Turkle observed some time ago, looking at computer screens causes a fragmentation of attention and identity, both of which are split between a number of windows.[55] From one window to another, from my Facebook page to my online banking website, I have neither the same identity nor the same personality; my passwords and behaviours are different. With digital technology, we are united to our surroundings not only by physical means, but also by electronic channels that are constantly growing in number. It is as if our identity and personality were divided within a continuum in which the boundary between the interior and exterior of our very selves is blurred.

Somalia Facebook: Gephi visualisation of the more than 1,000-friend Facebook network of a young Somali woman living in Nairobi, Kenya, in 2012
In the digital age, the diversity of online connections in which we are engaged echoes our inner multiplicity.

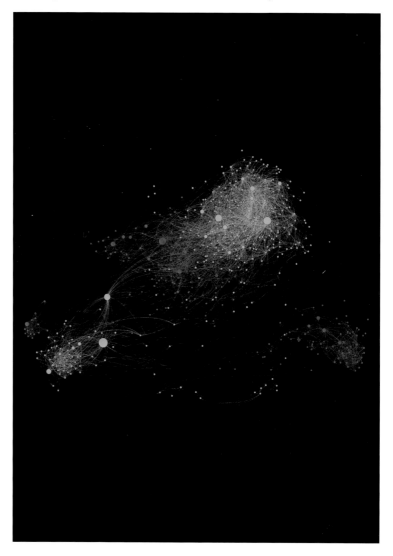

This blurring has a counterpart in the desire that we periodically feel to reassemble ourselves and in some sense to reconstruct the heroic figure: the sense of a unified self that would present itself to others in all its complexity but also in all its coherence. As the American communication specialists James Katz and Ronald Rice noted in the early 2000s, in counterpoint to Sherry Turkle's analyses, digital technology plays an essential role in this process of reconstruction.[56] Blogs and personal pages on Facebook, Viadeo and LinkedIn participate in such a process, just as much as do the countless digital photographs which we use constantly to document our lives and which we often post on Instagram. The current popularity of tattooing may

**Young Asian girl with nose and lip ring and tattoo**
The division of the self along multiple channels of online communication finds its counterpart in the reaffirmation of one's unique identity through means that include distinctive marks such as piercings and tattoos.

well stem from this same reconstruction project. Getting a tattoo is surely a way of affirming one's identity: a rather warlike identity that refuses to let itself dissolve into the surrounding urban jungle?

Perhaps the most fundamental contradiction of the digital individual lies in the dual trend of dispersal and concentration which seems to punctuate contemporary existence. The city carries the mark of this heartbeat in its entirety. It simultaneously embodies the ultimate location for dispersal, and one of the most favoured ways by which individuals can reassemble themselves. On the one hand, it reflects the multiplicity of channels through which individuality can be divided and expressed; on the other, by periodically forcing individuals to ask themselves where they are, what exactly they are doing and above all what they want, it forces them to reconstruct themselves. Taking the place of the flâneur, a typical figure in the major cities of the industrial era that the German philosopher Walter Benjamin sought to theorise, is a creature animated by a pulse that has it at one moment blending with its surroundings, and at the next reassembling itself, or at least attempting to gather itself together as a more compact entity.[57] But perhaps this alternation between fusion with the big city and a sense of separation was already a feature of the flâneur. In this case, would the digital individual represent nothing more than a new avatar of this city-dweller whose life depends on a certain number of foundational experiences such as this to-ing and fro-ing between fusion and separation? The frequency and intensity of the alternation between dispersal within an ever more diverse and split environment and concentration on oneself, however, suggests that the response to this question should be negative. Something profoundly new is being played out through the capacity of individuals to be at one with the city around them at certain moments, and to separate from it at others, later to melt back into it again.

It should be noted that the detour we have just taken through examining the question of the individual leads to a certain number of fundamental questions about the meaning that can be attributed to the term 'smart city'. First of all, the cyborg's inherent contradictions confirm the difficulty that a total surrender to neocybernetic temptation would present. It could not be a question of managing everything, even if it is possible to imagine more integrated management of certain urban systems that would link back to the old definition of the police as everything concerning public order, including in this category a certain number of tasks relating to sanitation and municipal government. This was for example the meaning given to the term by the

Parisian magistrate Nicolas Delamare in his monumental *Traité de la police* (*Treatise on the Police*), published in the early 18th century.[58] The Operations Center in Rio seems to illustrate a return to this pre-Revolutionary French understanding of the meaning of policing.

But such a return presents yet more limitations. Does that necessarily mean, however, that we need to rely on its absolute opposite: an ideal of spontaneity and organisation which is not without similarities to the Situationists' project of an urbanism that would liberate individuals' creative potential instead of mutilating them?[59] While the extraordinary capacity of individuals in the digital era to cooperate freely on ambitious projects should be acknowledged, their achievements still rarely threaten the position of institutional stakeholders. OpenStreetMap, for example, has not challenged the authority of Britain's Ordnance Survey or France's Institut Géographique National, and that is without even mentioning Google and Google Maps. Here again, the contemporary individual, who is neither entirely free nor completely held captive by large-scale public and private systems, seems to be evading overly simple scenarios. Between spontaneism with a flavour of utopia and neocybernetic temptation with a technocratic emphasis, more exploration is needed of what it means for digital individuals sometimes to be at one with their environment, which is a fundamentally urban one, and at other times to manage to extract themselves from it. On this model, a form of city intelligence needs to be conceived that is both widespread and focused, present in a diffuse way in the multiple interactions of its inhabitants with it and between themselves, and at the same time concentrated, at least partially, in control rooms, command posts and computer simulations intended for decision-making. It is necessary to get past this opposition between spontaneism and neocybernetic temptation in order to imagine successive levels of interaction between entities as diverse as physical infrastructure and computer programs, optimisation algorithms and cyborgs, and human–technology hybrids and individuals who alternate between fusion with their environment and reassembly at their core. Questions need to be asked as to the means by which these many levels could be coordinated, or even integrated within the overall activity of the city, offering an analogy with consciousness. Contemporary neuroscience can supply precious sources of inspiration in this respect. Some of its most eminent figures, such as the French specialist Stanislas Dehaene, see generalised stimulation of the cerebral cortex, comparable to a sort of ignition, as the most definite indication of conscious thought.[60] It may well be imagined that smart cities will one day experience a form of ignition.

# References

1 See Simon Sadler, *The Situationist City*, MIT Press (Cambridge, Massachusetts), 1998 and of course Henri Lefebvre, *Le Droit à la ville* [1968], Economica Anthropos (Paris), 2009.

2 On the dual character of the notion of event, see for instance François Dosse, *Renaissance de l'événement: Un défi pour l'historien – entre sphinx et phénix*, PUF (Paris), 2010.

3 Norbert Wiener, *Cybernetics, or Control and Communication in the Animal and the Machine*, Technology Press (Cambridge, Massachusetts), 1948. On cybernetics, see for instance Steve Joshua Heims, *Constructing a Social Science for Postwar America: The Cybernetics Group, 1946–1953*, MIT Press (Cambridge, Massachusetts), 1991.

4 Peter Galison, 'The Ontology of the Enemy: Norbert Wiener and the Cybernetic Vision', *Critical Inquiry*, vol 21, no 1, Autumn 1994, pp 228–66.

5 On the link between cybernetics and the cyborg, see Paul Edwards, *The Closed World: Computers and the Politics of Discourse in Cold War America*, MIT Press (Cambridge, Massachusetts), 1996, as well as Les Levidow and Kevin Robins (eds), *Cyborg Worlds: The Military Information Society*, Free Association Books (London), 1989.

6 Janice Hocker Rushing and Thomas S Frentz, *Projecting the Shadow: The Cyborg Hero in American Film*, Chicago University Press (Chicago and London), 1995.

7 They fascinated for instance the American architect and technology theorist Buckminster Fuller. They served as inspiration for his *World Game*, a simulation of the global operation of the earth using cybernetic notions. See Mark Wigley, 'Planetary Homeboy', *ANY Magazine*, no 17, 1997, pp 16–23.

8 Norbert Wiener was himself the co-author of an article on urban defence in the atomic age: Norbert Wiener, Karl Deutsch and Giorgio de Santillana, 'How US Cities Can Prepare for Atomic War: MIT Professors Suggest a Bold Plan to Prevent Panic and Limit Destruction', *Life*, 18 December 1950, pp 76–84.

On the context, which explains this publication, see Reinhold Martin, *The Organizational Complex: Architecture, Media, and Corporate Space*, MIT Press (Cambridge, Massachusetts), 2003.

9 Jennifer Light, *From Warfare to Welfare: Defense Intellectuals and Urban Problems in Cold War America*, Johns Hopkins University Press (Baltimore and London), 2003.

10 The project is described in Melville Campbell Branch, *Continuous City Planning: Integrating Municipal Management and City Planning*, John Wiley & Sons (New York), 1981.

11 Eden Medina, *Cybernetic Revolutionaries: Technology and Politics in Allende's Chile*, MIT Press (Cambridge, Massachusetts), 2011.

12 Natasha Singer, 'Mission Control, Built for Cities: IBM Takes "Smarter Cities" Concept to Rio de Janeiro', *New York Times*, 3 March 2012, http://www.nytimes.com/2012/03/04/business/ibm-takes-smarter-cities-concept-to-rio-de-janeiro.html (consulted 27 January 2015).

13 http://www.simudyne.com/

introduction-to-simudyne/
(consulted 5 February 2015).
On the relations between
Simudyne tools and computer
games, see Dan Grill, 'How
Games And Simulations
Will Save Us From Disaster',
*Rock, Paper, Shotgun*, 5
September 2014, http://
www.rockpapershotgun.
com/2014/09/05/how-
games-save-us-from-disaster/
(consulted 5 February 2015).
**14** 'Beyond The Quantified
Self: The World's Largest
Quantified Community',
http://www.fastcoexist.
com/3029255/beyond-the-
quantified-self-the-worlds-
largest-quantified-community
(consulted 12 February 2015).
**15** Christopher Alexander,
'A City is not a Tree', *Design*,
no 206, 1966, pp 46–55.
**16** Ray Kurzweil, *The
Singularity is Near: When
Humans Transcend Biology*,
Penguin (New York), 2005.
**17** Rory Cellan-Jones,
'Stephen Hawking Warns
Artificial Intelligence
Could End Mankind', *New
Technology*, 2 December
2014, http://www.bbc.com/
news/technology-30290540
(consulted 15 February 2015).

**18** Antoine Picon, *La Ville
territoire des cyborgs*, Les
Editions de l'Imprimeur
(Besançon), 1998.
**19** William J Mitchell, *Me++:
The Cyborg Self and the
Networked City*, MIT Press
(Cambridge, Massachusetts),
2003.
**20** Gregory Bateson, *Steps to
an Ecology of Mind: Collected
Essays in Anthropology,
Psychiatry, Evolution, and
Epistemology*, Chandler (San
Francisco), 1972.
**21** Matthew Gandy,
'Cyborg Urbanization:
Complexity and Monstrosity
in the Contemporary City',
*International Journal of Urban
and Regional Research*, vol 29,
no 1, March 2005, pp 26–49,
Erik Swyngedouw, 'Circulations
and Metabolisms: (Hybrid)
Natures and (Cyborg) Cities',
*Science as Culture*, vol 15, no
2, June 2006, pp 105–21.
**22** Michel Foucault, 'La
Naissance de la médecine
sociale' [1974–7], in *Dits et
écrits*, vol 2, Gallimard (Paris),
2001, pp 207–28.
**23** Marcus Ong, 'War on SARS:
A Singapore Experience',
*Canadian Journal of Emergency
Medicine*, vol 6, no 1, January

2004, pp 31–7.
**24** I was introduced to the
'Underworlds' project during a
visit to the SENSEable City Lab
on 3 June 2013.
**25** Sam Grobart, 'MC10's
BioStamp: The New Frontier of
Medical Diagnostics', 13 June
2013, http://www.bloomberg.
com/bw/articles/2013-06-13/
mc10s-biostamp-the-new-
frontier-of-medical-diagnostics
(consulted 3 February 2015).
**26** In Hollywood movies,
Terminator machines constitute
the only noteworthy exception
with their envelope made of
flesh that conceals a core made
of steel, plastic and silicon.
**27** Donna Haraway, 'A
Cyborg Manifesto: Science,
Technology, and Socialist
Feminism in the 1980s',
*Socialist Review*, vol 15, no 2,
1985, pp 65–107.
**28** Jean-François Chazerans,
'La Substance composée chez
Leibniz', *Revue philosophique
de la France et de l'étranger*,
vol 181, no 1, January–March
1991, pp 47–66.
**29** Dominique Cardon,
*La Démocratie Internet:
Promesses et limites*, Le Seuil
(Paris), 2010.
**30** *Smart London Plan*, http://

www.london.gov.uk/sites/default/files/smart_london_plan.pdf (consulted 12 February 2015).

**31** Antoine Picon, *Les Saint-simoniens: Raison, imaginaire et utopie*, Belin (Paris), 2002.

**32** Karl August Wittfogel, *Oriental Despotism: A Comparative Study of Total Power*, Yale University Press (New Haven), 1957.

**33** Howard Rheingold, *Smart Mobs: The Next Social Revolution*, Perseus (Cambridge, Massachusetts), 2003.

**34** See Habibul Haque Khondker, 'Role of the New Media in the Arab Spring', *Globalizations*, vol 8, no 5, October 2011, pp 675–9; and Gilad Lotan, Erhardt Graeff, Mike Ananny et al., 'The Revolutions Were Tweeted: Information Flows During the 2011 Tunisian and Egyptian Revolutions', *International Journal of Communication*, vol 5, 2011, pp 1375–405.

**35** http://wiki.openstreetmap.org/wiki/Stats (consulted 30 January 2015).

**36** http://www.fixmystreet.com/ (consulted 3 February 2015).

**37** https://www.waze.com/ (consulted 3 February 2015).

**38** Neil A Gershenfeld, *Fab: The Coming Revolution on Your Desktop – From Personal Computers to Personal Fabrication*, Basic Books (New York), 2005.

**39** 'Meu Rio: Where You Can Take Action!', http://transformbrazil.com/tag/meu-rio/ (consulted 3 February 2015).

**40** Anthony M Townsend, *Smart Cities: Big Data, Civic Hackers, and the Quest for a New Utopia*, WW Norton & Company (New York and London), 2013.

**41** http://mindmixer.com/ (consulted 3 February 2015).

**42** http://wiki.openstreetmap.org/wiki/Stats (consulted 30 January 2015).

**43** 'Wikipedia: Wikipedians', http://en.wikipedia.org/wiki/Wikipedia:Wikipedians (consulted 31 January 2015).

**44** R Stuart Geiger and David Ribes, 'The Work of Sustaining Order in Wikipedia: The Banning of a Vandal', *Proceedings of the 2010 ACM Conference on Computer Supported Cooperative Work (CSCW)*, New York, 2010, http://www.academia.edu/197709/The_Work_of_Sustaining_Order_in_Wikipedia_The_Banning_of_a_Vandal (consulted 3 February 2015); Aaron Halfaker and John Riedl, 'Bots and Cyborgs: Wikipedia's Immune System', *Computer*, vol 45, no 3, March 2012, pp 79–82; R Stuart Geiger and Aaron Halfaker, 'When the Levee Breaks: Without Bots, What Happens to Wikipedia's Quality Control Process?', http://stuartgeiger.com/wikisym13-cluebot.pdf (consulted 3 February 2015).

**45** Robert Ezra Park, *On Social Control and Collective Behavior*, Chicago University Press (Chicago), 1967, p 3.

**46** It constitutes for instance a central theme of Ulrich Beck, *Risk Society: Towards a New Modernity* [*Risikogesellschaft: Auf dem Weg in eine andere Moderne*, 1986], English translation, Sage (London), 1992.

**47** Nicholas Negroponte, *Being Digital*, Alfred A Knopf (New York), 1995.

**48** Michel Chevalier, *Lettres sur l'Amérique du Nord*, Charles Gosselin (Paris), 1836.

**49** Karl Marx, *Capital* [*Das*

*Kapital*, 1867], English translation, Penguin (Harmondsworth), 1990.
**50** Michael Hardt and Antonio Negri, *Empire*, Harvard University Press (Cambridge, Massachusetts), 2000.
**51** François de Singly (ed), *Famille et individualisation*, vol 1: *Être soi parmi les autres*, L'Harmattan (Paris), 2001; Patrice Flichy, *Le Sacre de l'amateur: Sociologie des passions ordinaires à l'ère numérique*, Le Seuil (Paris), 2010.
**52** Richard Powers, *The Echo Maker*, Picador (New York), 2006, p 190.
**53** Bateson 1972.
**54** See for instance Gilles Deleuze and Félix Guattari, *Anti-Oedipus: Capitalism and Schizophrenia* [*L'Anti-Oedipe*, 1973], English translation, University of Minnesota Press (Minneapolis), 1983; Gilles Deleuze and Félix Guattari, *A Thousand Plateaus: Capitalism and Schizophrenia* [*Mille Plateaux*, 1980], English translation, University of Minnesota (Minneapolis), 1987; Bruno Latour, *We Have Never Been Modern* [*Nous n'avons jamais été modernes*, 1991], English translation, Harvard University Press (Cambridge, Massachusetts), 1993; and Peter Sloterdijk, *Bubbles: Spheres Volume 1: Microspherology* [*Sphären I – Blasen, Mikrosphärologie*, 1998], English translation, Semiotext(e) (Los Angeles), 2011.
**55** Sherry Turkle, *Life on the Screen: Identity in the Age of the Internet*, Simon & Schuster (New York), 1995.
**56** James E Katz and Ronald E Rice, *Social Consequences of Internet Use: Access, Involvement, and Interaction*, MIT Press (Cambridge, Massachusetts), 2002. On this reconstruction of the self, see also Antonio A Casilli, *Les Liaisons numériques: Vers une Nouvelle sociabilité?*, Le Seuil (Paris), 2010.
**57** Walter Benjamin, *The Arcades Project* [*Das Passagen-Werk*, 1982], English translation, Belknap Press of Harvard University (Cambridge, Massachusetts), 1999.
**58** Nicolas Delamare, *Traité de la police*, Jean et Pierre Cot (Paris), 1705–10.
**59** Sadler 1998.
**60** Stanislas Dehaene, *Consciousness and the Brain: Deciphering How the Brain Codes Our Thoughts*, Viking (New York), 2014.

# 3

# Urban Intelligence, Space and Maps

The smart city is not an ethereal entity, in the manner of a spirit floating above the streets and buildings. It has by necessity a localised character, inseparable from the physical environment within which its inhabitants evolve. Two key technologies – augmented reality and geolocation – allow a better understanding of this inseparability of atoms of matter from data bits. City intelligence must again be envisaged as profoundly spatial, even if, as we will see later in this chapter, the impact of information and communications technology on urban form is not obvious as yet.

Despite these uncertainties, it is still possible to venture some hypotheses concerning the evolution of the physical framework of cities, starting with the decreasing relevance of the compositional logic that has long dominated urban design, and the new importance of interior spaces that allow improved monitoring of environmental parameters. If we add to this a new relationship with infrastructure that is less dependent on the device of the network, the urban ideal that is finally revealing itself is noticeably different from the industrial city that was organised purely around flow management.

Mapping is playing an essential role in the emergence of smart cities. This brings us back to what neuroscience has to tell us, this time concerning neural maps without which there could be no conscious activity.[1] It is because of its ability to draw up maps of the body of which it forms an integral part, as well as of its environment, memories and, in the case of humans, all sorts of notions and ideas of varying levels of abstraction, that the brain can learn, understand and reason. In the urban realm, the emergence of new mapping practices may be a prelude to the formation of an unprecedented type of collective intelligence that brings together humans and non-humans, algorithms and cyborgs.

## Augmented Reality and Geolocation

Two technological developments have proved fundamental in the rise of cities based on connected systems, individuals and structures that can be considered as intelligent. The first resides in a growing association between the physical and the digital world, or between atoms and data bits, which is often referred to as 'augmented reality'. Inseparable from this, the second relates to the predominance of geolocation techniques.

The notion of augmented reality can be defined more or less broadly. Here we will adopt its most widely accepted meaning, which concerns the formation of 'hybrid ecologies', to use an expression employed by the British computer scientists Andy Crabtree and Tom Rodden in a 2008 article.[2] While the presence of screens in physical space constitutes one of the most immediately identifiable forms of augmented reality, there are many other ways of uniting atoms and bits, such as the presence of wireless networks and, more generally, the association between spatial sequences and digital resources that is at the origin of ubiquitous computing.

The era has passed when the virtual was opposed to the real and seemed to threaten its stability. The link between atoms and bits has become banal, and refers to a range of aims, including civic projects to make useful information available to the public, and commercial and educational motives, without mentioning the contribution that augmented reality makes to the control of complex systems and to scientific research. Through the range of information that is displayed on fixed and mobile screens, from the digital terminals installed by municipal authorities – such as the interactive panels of Urbanflow in Helsinki or LinkNYC in New York – to smartphones that enrich their users' interpretation of their immediate environment, augmented reality has begun to change public space.[3] It offers a whole array of applications related to tourism. For example, a few years ago the town of Cluny in Burgundy, eastern France, trialled screens that allowed visitors walking around the ruins of its abbey church to visualise the Romanesque building as it was in its heyday.[4]

While screens and digital image projections on walls and objects still occupy a dominant position within augmented reality, ubiquitous computing may well help to reduce the inclination to resort to them systematically. Google Glass has started to challenge their claim to supremacy. It is possible to imagine a world in which electronic content infiltrates almost all matter, cities where views and atmospheres appear as tangled confusions of atoms and data bits. The exact nature of the technologies that will precipitate this development is not particularly important to our subject. It is perhaps more crucial to recognise how much this increasing hybridisation between physical space and digital content will contribute to the further spread of the dynamic in which individuals are dispersed within rich and diverse

environments. This may well seem alarming; but it is worth noting the extent to which this evolution is anchored in the deepest recesses of our contemporary condition as individuals who are ever more connected and thus even inseparable from our surroundings.

Geolocation constitutes the other key technology. Thanks to techniques such as satellite positioning as used in the American-initiated GPS (global positioning system), which may soon be challenged by Europe's Galileo system, and triangulation via mobile phone masts, it is possible to determine the position occupied by a growing number of objects and individuals, both stationary and on the move. These can be applied in countless ways: from the transport to the tracking of a nomadic workforce; from contextualised service offers based on one's current location, to the possibility already presented by networks such as Facebook to know which of one's friends are in one's immediate vicinity.[5]

Augmented-reality terminals showing a reconstitution of the church of Cluny, Cluny, Burgundy, France, 2011
The abbey church of Cluny, one of the largest Romanesque churches ever built, was almost completely destroyed at the beginning of the 19th century. In cooperation with the engineering school Arts et Métiers ParisTech, the city of Cluny has tested the use of augmented-reality terminals enabling visitors to visualise the church as it was prior to its destruction.

Geolocation has fascinated artists from the outset. In 1995, the American architect, designer and educator Laura Kurgan recorded her movements for the purposes of an exhibition at the Museum of Contemporary Art in Barcelona entitled 'You Are Here'.[6] Later, between 2003 and 2010, the British artist Daniel Belasco Rogers used a GPS to map all of his journeys in Berlin. Revealingly named 'The Drawing of my Life', the project generated a series of maps obtained by superimposing records of different journeys, from 'One Year Drawing Berlin' to 'Seven Years Drawing Berlin'.[7]

The autobiographical dimension that such projects often assume is by no means accidental. The blue dot that gently pulsates on the screen in your

Laura Kurgan, 'You Are Here' project, nine points, two lines, and five letters, stationary and mobile GPS receiver on roof above Museu d'Art Contemporani de Barcelona, 1 September 1995
Using GPS technology, artist Laura Kurgan began to explore the moving threshold between physical and digital made possible by geolocation in the mid-1990s.

92.68m

0

88.55m

YOU ARE HERE: MUSEU  Nine points, two lines, and five letters,
stationary and mobile GPS receiver on roof above Museu d'Art Contemporani de Barcelona.

Data: 3079 position records, after differential correction.
Acquired: 1 September 1995, in nine separate sequences, 09:48:13- 15:30:13 GPS time,
and 2 September 1995, in seven separate sequences, 09:10:36 - 10:30:14 GPS time.
NAVSTAR satellites seen: 04, 07, 14, 18, 15, 28, 21, 01, 23, 22, 31

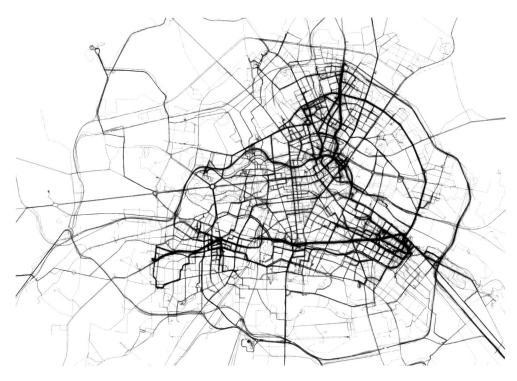

mobile phone's Google Maps app, like a sort of primordial event from which everything else proceeds, takes you to the physical limits of the flesh and bone of your body as well as to the exact spot where it is located: 'You are here.' From this starting point of concentrated identity, it becomes possible to investigate the locations of underground railway stations, shops, or nearby places where you are planning to meet your friends. Inseparable from augmented reality, and based on its most strategic applications, geolocation occasionally reminds the individuals of the digital era that they can also distinguish themselves from their surroundings, and reassemble themselves, even if only for an instant, before stretching out – or unfolding themselves, to borrow a Deleuzian metaphor – towards their environment.[8]

**Daniel Belasco Rogers, 'All My Journeys in Berlin 2003–2013', 2013**
With this type of enterprise using again GPS technology, the map of the city becomes profoundly autobiographical.

## Towards Three-Dimensional Urbanism

Up to now, the development of information and communications technology and smart city projects has not had any obvious impact on the spatial structure of cities. A couple of decades ago, William J Mitchell judged that the time had come to announce the advent of a 'soft city', where electronic exchanges would take the place of physical meetings.[9] This was not to be, however: instead, the rise of e-mail and e-commerce resulted in an intensification of vehicular and pedestrian traffic in the urban arena. Around the same time, several prophets of the digital era visualised a movement of urban decentralisation on a scale comparable to that provoked by the car, since many sorts of activities that had hitherto taken place in city centres could now be relocated.[10] Here again, the evolution of metropolises has given the lie to their scenarios. From London to Hong Kong, Singapore and Tokyo, the importance of dense urban centres has shown a tendency to be reinforced under the effect of factors such as the financialisation of the economy. In this context, it is not surprising that the world's 50 largest cities are home to almost half of all websites.[11]

So, urban forms have changed little. Unlike the car, digital technology does not seem to have had an immediate impact on road networks or on the size of buildings. Its effects have been more similar to those of electricity in the years around 1900: a profound transformation of the experience of the city rather than of its physical structure. Of course, architecture has undergone far-reaching changes in the same period. New forms of geometry have appeared, along with the spread of a return to ornament that has helped bring about the new urban sensuality discussed in chapter 1.[12] From giant

**Solar-powered Soofa bench, 2014**
Digital technology and augmented reality have already begun to transform street furniture. The bench not only enables the charging of smartphones; it also senses its surroundings to provide information about environmental conditions such as air quality.

screens to digital projections onto building facades, augmented reality enriches architecture's effects on public space. It also manifests itself in the apparition of innovative street furniture, such as the benches currently being tested by the Soofa company in Cambridge, Massachusetts, that use solar energy to charge up mobile phones and tablets, or the amazing eTree created by the Israeli firm Sologic, likewise powered by solar panels. The eTree offers a shady shelter in the daytime, and light at night; it provides access to Wi-Fi and again features sockets for charging mobile phones.[13] Solar panels and green roofs are starting to modify the general silhouette of buildings both in city centres and in the suburbs. But this set of evolutions leaves the general fabric of cities unchanged, at least for the time being.

Nothing is more revealing in this respect than the essentially rather classical character of the urban forms adopted for new 'smart' cities and districts. Whether it be in 22@Barcelona, the Catalan metropolis's flagship project in terms of the integration of information and communications technology, or in the new towns of Masdar and Songdo, formal inventiveness is not the priority, and references to existing forms proliferate. So the promoters of Songdo set out to borrow boulevards from Paris, the Central Park principle from New York and canals from Venice.[14]

eTree prototype by Sologic installed in the Ramat Hanadiv park, Zichron Ya'akov, Israel, 2014 Designed by artist Yoav Ben-Dov, the eTree appears both as a sculpture with its metal tubes that imitate the branches of a tree and as a piece of urban furniture that connects to the digital world.

Foster + Partners, Masdar City masterplan, Abu Dhabi, UAE, 2008
A sustainable and smart new town designed for 45,000 to 50,000 people in Abu Dhabi, Masdar appears as the inheritor of a long tradition of grid street plans, from Ancient Greek colonies to 19th-century American cities.

All of this does not necessarily mean that physical space does not matter any more. On the contrary: the sentient and sensual city, augmented reality and geolocation enhance every square metre of urban space, investing it with new and unexpected functionalities and meanings. Even more importantly, through connected individuals and sensors, city intelligence seems to be present everywhere, like a sort of fluid that could give urban structures access to a higher level of existence. We are witnessing not so much the transformation of these structures, but rather their reinterpretation.

In his *Essais de physique* (*Essays on Physics*), the 17th-century French doctor, scholar and architect Claude Perrault pictured the souls of living creatures as spread over every part of their bodies, instead of residing in the pineal gland as René Descartes had proposed.[15] The smart city might be imagined as a sort of marriage between Perrault's and Descartes's concepts, allowing the city's intelligence to be simultaneously diffuse, ubiquitous, and concentrated in certain places such as the regulation and control rooms of major technological systems.

At the consummation of this marriage, the fabric of the city – its flesh, if you will – is not only reinterpreted, but also in some sense transfigured. As we will soon see, it is true that mapping in its broadest sense constitutes both one of the favoured procedures for this transfiguration and the analyser that allows its essential issues to be understood. The importance of mapping can be summarised by saying that, to date, it is not so much the form of the city that has changed, but more its map, or rather maps, given the extent to which the advent of digital technology has coincided with a proliferation of mapped representations of the urban phenomenon. It is through this proliferation that the city appears intelligent.

The profoundly spatial character of this intelligence urges us not to stop at merely acknowledging an evolution of urban form that is yet to occur, but to seek out the precursory signs of change in the phenomena that are before our very eyes. The rise of mapping does not mean that the physical framework of the city has no need to change in the future. On the

**General view of Songdo International Business District, Incheon, South Korea**
Traditional urban references are equally present in Songdo, from a system of pocket parks based on the design of Savannah, Georgia, to canals like those of Venice. Built on 600 hectares (1,500 acres) of reclaimed land along the Yellow Sea, the city aims to be a model for sustainable city-scale development. One of its objectives is to reach 40 per cent of water recycling and 76 per cent of waste recycling by 2020.

High-rise buildings along
Songdo main park,
Incheon, South Korea,
2013
Central Park in New York
is clearly a reference here.
The quest for smart and
sustainable cities has not yet
given birth to radically new
urban forms.

contrary: one of the consequences of the proliferation of maps, beginning
with the background that most smartphones can display to indicate their
owner's position via the aforementioned blue dot, effectively consists in
extensive decrease of the importance of regularity in urban form as a means
of orientation in space. It is not necessary to be faced with vast views or
surrounded by rigorously organised squares in order to identify the place
where one is located. However important it may be, the process of physically
locating oneself is now merely one of the dimensions of a presence which
is also played out on the level of digital content. Continuous practical
experience of augmented reality deeply transforms our understanding of
space. This results in the possibility, which is only just starting to be glimpsed
by some urbanists and architects, of totally rethinking urban form in a
way unbounded by traditional compositional logic. There is no longer an
inevitable need for a regular two-dimensional framework that functions in
the manner of a simplified plan. More complex or even labyrinthine forms
are now permissible, with overlapping or tangled masses along the lines of
some vernacular dwellings. This liberation from compositional shackles that
have become less and less crucial may well generate a truly three-dimensional

type of urbanism. While it does not necessarily involve a rekindling of the megastructural utopias that typified the 1950s and 1960s, with their cities of the future conceived as gigantic edifices often formed by amassing identical modules within an abnormally enlarged structural framework, it does entail asking questions about the city more openly than urban planners and urban designers have done over the last few decades, whether they were faithful to the principles of Modernism or, on the contrary, tempted by the theories of New Urbanism, that offspring of Postmodernism which tries to resurrect traditional neighbourhood design.[16] The triumph of urban mapping invites us to leave ground-plan-based urbanism definitively behind us, whatever our ideological affiliation.

View of Jodhpur, Rajasthan, India, 2011
With the possible abandonment of two-dimensional regularity, the development of smart cities could eventually lead to the rediscovery of the spatial complexity of traditional vernacular urban forms.

Although urban forms have still changed little, a new area of freedom has been opened up by the advent of cities that are inseparably both physical and digital. Without waiting for the urbanists, various architectural firms have begun to explore the new possibilities that are being presented to them. From Herzog & de Meuron to Scott Cohen to OMA, over the past few years they have tested, for example, the stacking of volumes, representing a radical shift from the techniques of architectural composition that put the two-dimensional plan first.[17]

Complexity, entanglement, three-dimensionality; in addition to these development perspectives for urban forms that are different from the ones we already know, there is also an inclination to accord ever greater importance to interiors – whether they be in residential blocks, shopping centres or airports – to the detriment of considerations of outside space. Increasingly large segments of cities are appearing as though they were merely successions of interiors. Several factors have supported this tendency. Firstly, there is the desire for spatial control that is linked sometimes to security needs, sometimes to the pursuit of commercial viability. In today's capitalist societies, isolation has become desirable, whether to protect ourselves or to carry on our business. More recently, questions relating to the control of atmospheric conditions and the quest for improved environmental quality have begun to come into play. They are expressed in their most extreme form through hypothetical proposals such as the Belgian architect Julien De Smedt's Shenzhen Logistic City (begun 2006), and earlier in the

OMA, The Interlace, Singapore, 2009
Stacking is among the techniques that enable contemporary architects to imagine a different, more intricate mode of living in cities. With The Interlace, the aim was to conceive the development as a three-dimensional network of housing and social spaces integrated with the natural environment.

Italian architect Paolo Soleri's proposals for residential developments that are simultaneously dense and environmentally friendly, for which he coined the term 'Arcology' (a contraction of 'architecture and 'ecology') in the late 1960s.[18] Even more than the monumentality of the exterior, it is the importance accorded to the interior spaces that is the most striking aspect of the Shenzhen Logistic City, a true Arcology of the digital era.

The proliferation of what the French sociologist Dominique Lorrain calls *paquebots urbains* ('urban liners'), which he defines as 'large-scale developments that can function as autonomous worlds, offering their occupants/clients all the facilities of the modern world' – in other words as massive interiors – does not only concern advanced industrial countries.[19] They are also appearing in increasing numbers in the metropolises of the developing world, in order to counterbalance the degradation of public space and the lack of reliable supplies of resources such as water and electricity.

To the extent that it relies on a desire for increased control of the urban metabolism, the smart city will accelerate this process of interiorisation of entire sections of the city. This tendency is in danger of accentuating the logic of fragmentation that has already characterised large contemporary cities for

Julien De Smedt,
Shenzhen Logistic City,
2006, general view and
interior perspective
Gigantism is not necessarily
the most salient aspect
of this project, even if its
proposed 1,111 metres of
height would have dwarfed
the 828 metres of the Burj
Khalifa tower in Dubai. The
ambition to design a truly
three-dimensional city is
perhaps more significant.
Equally revealing is the
accent put on interior
public spaces somewhat
reminiscent of the ambience
of gallerias and shopping
malls, as if the future of
the city were to be both
interiorised and privatised.

quite some time. Neither the major networks inherited from the 19th century nor traditional techniques of urban composition have managed to fight effectively against this process. It is therefore all the more urgent to rethink urbanism on the basis of the possibilities offered by an association between the physical environment and electronic content; and, while doing so, to seek qualities of complexity and entanglement that could serve as a counterpoint to the phenomenon of ever more inward-looking living spaces.

## A New Relationship to Infrastructure

In many ways, the smart city is the successor of the networked city, organised around flows, which emerged in the course of the 19th century. But at the same time it stands apart from it and indeed shakes up some of its key aspects. The importance within the development of the smart city of monitoring events, at the expense of the exclusive emphasis on flow management, has already been underlined in the previous chapter. A few additional elements now need to be examined, outlining a different relationship to infrastructure which does not automatically involve summoning up the notion of networks as it did before.

Imagination and concrete practices support each other in this evolution. Let us begin with the imaginary in arguably its most paradoxical form: that of the disconnection that appears possible, or even vital, within an ever more connected world. This concept has long thrived in the cataclysmic vision that has been popularised by numerous fictional works, novels and films. Within the post-apocalyptic world depicted in such works, survival often depends on the capacity to live without networks, whether the latter are controlled by hostile forces or have simply disappeared. Such a vision is also the successor of the theme of 'off-the-grid' living to which a whole series of alternative movements subscribed in the 1960s and 1970s. It is significant that some of these movements played an essential role in the history of digital technology by contributing to the advent of micro-computing, in the hope of freeing computer users from their dependence on large-scale integrated systems. Digital technology has already been linked for a long time with both networks and a desire for self-sufficiency or even disconnection. Today we are witnessing a major development of this vision, in relation to the problems that are posed by energy transition. Urban schemes such as BedZED (2002), the Peabody Trust's pioneering 'zero-energy development' of homes and

**Bill Dunster, BedZED, London, 2002**
BedZED, for Beddington Zero Energy Development, was among the very first large-scale communities designed to achieve zero carbon emission. Using far less energy than a conventional development, it is based on an ideal of self-sufficiency that challenges the conventional approach of the city based on interdependency.

workspaces in north London, offer a no less than spectacular reduction of the dependence of buildings on traditional urban supply networks.[20] On a more general level, it is hard not to be struck by the propensity of positive-energy buildings and eco-neighbourhoods to be conceived as isolated entities that are partially disconnected from urban infrastructure. They thus contribute to the aforementioned fragmentation of the urban organism.

The theme of disconnection falls within a group of contemporary questions on the perverse effects of classical grids and networks such as drains, which tend to generate environmental problems at their periphery. In order to avoid such issues, one of the solutions may consist in a move towards more localised forms of technological systems that would make less of an impact on the environment and above all allow the harmful effects to be diminished through symbiosis, with the waste produced by one element of the system being reused by another element. This type of alternative to traditional

**Core eco-cycles of the Hammarby Sjöstad model**
A former harbour area in Stockholm, the Hammarby Sjöstad area has been transformed into an eco-friendly city quarter since 1990. From energy production to water consumption, and from heating to waste management, the emphasis is put on local synergies rather than systematic dependence upon larger urban networks.

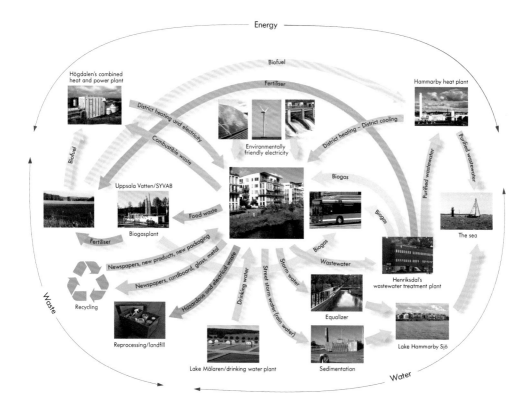

networks has been trialled in several of the Nordic countries. It forms the basis of what is sometimes called the Hammarby Sjöstad model, named after a district of Stockholm where its application is particularly advanced.[21]

Furthermore, the advent of digital technology has tended to render the workings of some infrastructures more independent of their perceptions as networks than before. This is particularly true of transport infrastructure. With GPS, the notion of a specific itinerary tends to take precedence over that of finding one's way in reference to the structure of the road network. Whether one is on a back street, a minor road, a major road or a motorway is of little importance. What matters now is the place of a given sequence within a series that is indifferent to the logic of road networks and their various components.

This development has of course been made possible by the availability to drivers via GPS of far greater quantities of information than traditional maps can provide. The phenomenon is even more evident in the realm of urban travel. All over the world, passenger information systems announce the number of minutes remaining before the arrival of the next underground train. Many bus networks likewise supply this sort of information, which passengers can use to help them judge whether it is worth waiting for the next bus or train. With smartphones, resourceful people can even devise more complex strategies, combining bus and train, bicycle and car. City-dwellers will ultimately be less and less limited by a single network that

View of countdown clock sign at Lorimer Street station, Brooklyn, New York City Subway, 2013
The ability to know in real time when the next trains are to arrive opens up new possibilities for travellers.

leaves them no choice but to patiently await the next bus or train, with no guarantees beyond a timetable that is often more theoretical than it is real.

Transport offers have started to change as a consequence. The rise of car-sharing clubs and taxi networks such as Zipcar and Uber, established in the United States in 2000 and 2009 respectively and now operating in countries around the world, falls within this context, as does the proliferation of self-service vehicle systems such as Paris's Vélib', set up in 2007, and London's cycle hire scheme, popularly known as 'Boris Bikes' after Boris Johnson, the mayor at the time of their introduction in 2010. Also worth mentioning are experiments such as the Bridj buses in Boston, launched in 2014, whose timetables adapt in real time to their users' needs on the basis of millions of data on commuter journeys collected from sites such as Google Earth, Facebook, Foursquare, Twitter and LinkedIn.[22] After entering the desired departure and arrival points in a smartphone app, Bridj users are assigned pick-up and drop-off points. Through contact with data mining practices and making use of the possibilities of interaction with users that are offered by smartphones, the designers of transport systems are thus exploring new directions that lead to solutions which are more flexible than traditional networks.

Are we definitively at the point of witnessing a reconsideration of the networked city that we inherited from the industrial era? Even if the enthusiasm that surrounds some of the current experiments ought to be tempered, the question still needs to be asked. As is demonstrated by the

**Vélib' bicycles in Paris, 2011**
Digital technology is instrumental in the workings of the new self-service vehicle systems that are spreading all over the world. A trip can now include a segment on the metro or the bus and another riding a rented bicycle or car.

Boarding for a Bridj bus to downtown Boston from Brookline, Massachusetts, 2014
The traditional interpretation of urban transport systems as networks is being challenged by services such as the Boston-area Bridj buses, the routes of which do not follow fixed patterns but adapt to the overall rhythms of the city as well as to customers' demands through data mining and a smartphone interface.

example of BedZED, a project that is in reality far from being fully self-sufficient in terms of energy and which requires London's electricity grid to satisfy demand at certain peak periods, it is necessary to be effectively connected in order to be able to live outside the network for part of the time.

Above all, it is important not to fall into an indiscriminate apologia for the beneficial effects of innovation. The questioning of the notion of networks that is happening in fields from sanitation to transport as a result of information and communications technology may well lead to cities becoming even more fragmented. This is at least the hypothesis that the British geographers Stephen Graham and Simon Marvin defended in a 2001 book tellingly entitled *Splintering Urbanism*.[23] The developments that urban mapping has undergone over the last few decades need to be interpreted as a counterpoint to this worrying tendency. Whether produced by institutions, businesses or individuals, new maps of the city effectively represent a major element of integration, the surest sign that a new form of urban intelligence is currently emerging.

## The Stakes of Representation

Over the last few decades, urban mapping has seen a spectacular set of developments.[24] Firstly, it has undergone an explosion in volume. At the same time, the notion of the map has broadened in line with the shift from paper to screen: from GPS terminals in cars to mobile phones, most of the maps we consult these days are presented in the form of pixels.[25] Upstream from this, mapping is made possible by databases of geolocation information which is again growing exponentially. This increased dependence of mapping on computerised data is at the root of geographic information systems (GIS) which allow the gathering of information on not only topography, natural resources, land parcels, infrastructure and buildings, but also the values of all sorts of environmental, social, political, cultural and commercial parameters. Still, GIS is only the institutional side of an abundant production that relies on the use of open applications, better known as API (application programming interfaces), such as Google Maps, which is used by more than 2,300,000 websites around the world.[26] Google Maps allows a full array of stakeholders – individuals, associations, small and large businesses – to locate the data that interest them on a map. Long the preserve of professionals, mapping has not escaped the movement of democratisation, albeit relative, that Patrice Flichy has described as the 'consecration of the amateur' (see chapter 2).[27]

The shift from paper to screen effectively changes the paper map into a mere printout comparable to that of a document that is constantly evolving. It allows mapping to become dynamic, updateable either automatically or on demand, zoomable and/or clickable; in a word, interactive. In the control rooms and neocybernetics-inspired simulation programs of the smart city that are emerging before our very eyes, such maps allow us to keep track, often in real time, of what is happening within technological systems and infrastructures, energy grids, water and sanitation systems, road networks and public transport. Rendering what happens visible, they are linked to control panels and allow operators to intervene in order to regulate or resolve crisis situations. As Bruno Latour observed in his 1998 essay *Paris ville invisible* (*Paris, Invisible City*), describing the control room of the Parisian water authority SAGEP, they represent a sort of modern equivalent to the Panopticon, the institutional building form devised by the British social theorist Jeremy Bentham in the late 18th century to allow a single watchman to observe all inmates without them knowing.[28] Earlier I mentioned the spread of the model of mapping; as maps have passed from paper to screen, the dividing line between mapping and surveillance is fading, or even disappearing completely in many cases. The most spectacular urban visualisations produced by the SENSEable City Lab at MIT illustrate this blurring of boundaries. For example, the animation *Real Time Rome*, presented at the Venice Architecture Biennale in 2006, offers an arresting

image of the evolution of the spatial distribution and number of calls
made from mobile phones during events such as the football World Cup
in 2006, or a concert given by Madonna in the Italian capital in the same
year.[29] This animation relies on the possibility of knowing the position of the
phones' holders at every moment, through triangulation between masts.
The gathering of these data by the phone operator Telecom Italia, together
with their processing by the SENSEable City Lab, could be compared to
a form of surveillance. *Real
Time Rome* provides a general,
almost panoptic view of what
is happening on the street. In
*New York Talk Exchange*, shown
at the Museum of Modern Art
in New York in 2008, which
offers a visual representation
of destinations and volumes of
telephone calls and information
exchanges on the Internet
generated by trading activity at
the New York Stock Exchange,
the boundary between mapping
and surveillance is just as
porous.[30] The success of this

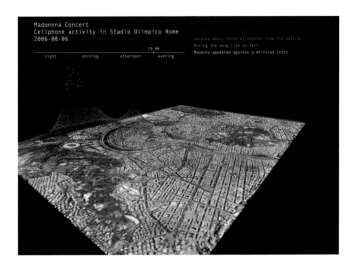

MENU   SELECT   BUILDINGS   ENERGY   TRANSPORT   ROAD   ENVIRONMENT   CUSTOM   POWER   ROUTING   HEAT MAPS   RISK PROFILES   MEASURE   LINE OF SIGHT

**Cityzenith demo of new release of the 5D Smart City data visualisation platform in Barcelona, Spain, November 2014**
A cloud-based software, the Cityzenith platform aims to map the massive amounts of data created by cities. In Barcelona, the implementation of the platform will dovetail with the city's effort to develop its own master database in order to improve communication among municipal agencies.

type of visualisation, as witnessed by the increasing numbers of similar undertakings such as those produced by Orange and FABERNOVEL using Urban Mobs technology, again harks back to the neocybernetic temptation to see, predict and monitor better.[31]

In recent years, the tools for urban visualisation intended to facilitate such monitoring have increased in number, often hand in hand with the proliferation of urban data. The Cityzenith platform, for example, offers cities tools to allow them to harness all sorts of information – open data, Internet of Things, machine to machine and social media – to assist decision-making.[32] Visualisation and simulation are never far apart; the Synthicity platform, for example, inextricably mixes the two together.[33]

A possibility of switching almost continuously between the overall city scale and that of individual behaviours often features among the new elements that are introduced with these multiple experiments and tools. But the individuals and groups that they freely form produce other maps which constitute a sort of antidote to this desire for control. The mapping program 'iSee' is emblematic in this regard. Made available online by the Institute for Applied Autonomy, an organisation that claims to be 'dedicated to the cause of individual and collective self-determination', it allows users to outsmart the surveillance of video cameras installed in Manhattan. Once the user has entered points of departure and arrival, 'iSee' proposes an itinerary that enables him or her to avoid being featured in video recordings.[34]

Other maps containing more militant content rely on data made available by administrative bodies and businesses within the context of open data. By combining the last declared home addresses of American prisoners with the cost of their incarceration, Laura Kurgan has managed, for example, to produce maps showing the spatial distribution of 'million-dollar blocks': residential blocks from which criminals emerge in sufficient numbers that the cost of their imprisonment exceeds a million dollars.[35]

While Kurgan's aim is to make people think about the relationship between urban environment and criminality and about the cost of the latter, the majority of maps produced outside the confines of official institutions place more emphasis on sharing information and experiences. This might involve collective information and experiences, obtained through techniques such as crowdsourcing, or an individual experience that a person wants to make accessible to others. We may want to share 'our' city, just as we share certain moments of our lives on social media. While the representation of what is happening within large-scale technological systems is meant to be perfectly objective, many of these maps, and especially those that are created by individuals, mix objective elements with decidedly subjective comments. What happens to me is almost always presented as a continuum of events that can be observed by others together with personal feelings and emotions. Such a continuum is not without similarities to the principles of 'psychogeographical drifting' that the Situationists, led by Guy Debord, attempted to map, as if the ultimate issue of true urbanism consisted in spotting the locations that 'objectively' offer a potential for producing sensations and emotions.[36] Making use of digital tools for geolocation, recording of the urban environment and detection of levels of psychological stimulation, a number of artists have set out to work at the crossroads between mapping and the sensual and emotional potential of certain urban sequences. This is particularly the case of Christian Nold and his 'emotion maps' of Greenwich, San Francisco and the east of Paris, which are successors to Guy Debord's ventures.[37]

Screenshot of the 'iSee' tool developed by the Institute for Applied Autonomy, 2015
The application allows the user to determine which itinerary is the best between two locations in Manhattan to avoid as much as possible being tracked by video surveillance cameras.

Laura Kurgan, 'Architecture and Justice, Million Dollar Blocks' project, 17 'million dollar blocks' in Brownsville, Brooklyn, based on data from 2003
Started in 2005, the 'Million Dollars Blocks' project uses data visualisation in an innovative and militant way to foster reflection on the American penitentiary system and some of its underlying urban causes. The map presents itself as an inversion of the usual cartography of criminal hot spots by mapping the home addresses of people admitted to prison.

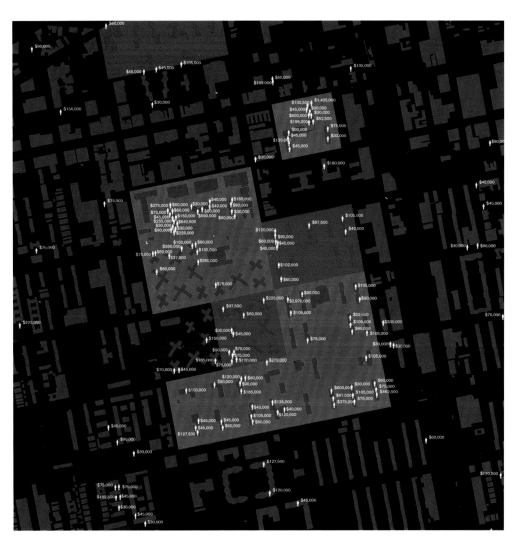

**BROWNSVILLE,
BROOKLYN**

IT COST 17 MILLION DOLLARS TO IMPRISON
109 PEOPLE FROM THESE 17 BLOCKS
IN 2003. WE CALL THESE MILLION DOLLAR
BLOCKS. ON A FINANCIAL SCALE
PRISONS ARE BECOMING THE
PREDOMINANT GOVERNING INSTITUTION
IN THE NEIGHBORHOOD.

Percent Persons of Color, 2000.

Percent Persons Below Poverty Level, 2000.

Percent Adults Admitted to Prison, 2003.

| BROOKLYN COMMUNITY DISTRICTS | % POPULATION | % POVERTY | % ADMISSIONS |
|---|---|---|---|
| BROOKLYN CD 1 | 6.51 % | 9.08 % | 5.27 % |
| BROOKLYN CD 2 | 4.03 % | 3.58 % | 4.64 % |
| BROOKLYN CD 3 | 5.83 % | 6.10 % | 15.51 % |
| BROOKLYN CD 4 | 4.24 % | 6.34 % | 9.34 % |
| BROOKLYN CD 5 | 7.04 % | 9.30 % | 14.45 % |
| BROOKLYN CD 6 | 4.25 % | 2.60 % | 3.08 % |
| BROOKLYN CD 7 | 5.03 % | 5.03 % | 3.82 % |
| BROOKLYN CD 8 | 3.79 % | 4.15 % | 9.49 % |
| BROOKLYN CD 9 | 4.25 % | 4.14 % | 4.43 % |
| BROOKLYN CD 10 | 4.96 % | 2.79 % | 0.91 % |
| BROOKLYN CD 11 | 7.05 % | 5.54 % | 1.26 % |
| BROOKLYN CD 12 | 7.39 % | 6.64 % | 1.32 % |
| BROOKLYN CD 13 | 4.23 % | 4.94 % | 3.41 % |
| BROOKLYN CD 14 | 6.19 % | 6.22 % | 3.79 % |
| BROOKLYN CD 15 | 6.48 % | 4.43 % | 1.20 % |
| BROOKLYN CD 16 | 3.49 % | 5.02 % | 5.43 % |
| BROOKLYN CD 17 | 6.76 % | 5.40 % | 5.29 % |
| BROOKLYN CD 18 | 7.98 % | 3.91 % | 3.20 % |
| BROOKLYN TOTAL | 100.00 % | 100.00 % | 100.00 % |

Comparisons Expressed as Percent of Borough Total.

Prisoner Migration with Expenditures by Block, 2003.

**BROOKLYN, NEW YORK CITY**

**ADDED UP BLOCK BY BLOCK, IT COST $359 MILLION DOLLARS TO IMPRISON PEOPLE FROM BROOKLYN IN 2003, FACILITATING A MASS MIGRATION TO PRISONS IN UPSTATE NEW YORK. 95% EVENTUALLY RETURN HOME.**

Laura Kurgan, 'Architecture and Justice, Million Dollar Blocks' project, prisoner migration patterns, Brooklyn, New York, based on data from 2003
Another striking visualisation, this time of the migration between home and prison of people living in Brooklyn. On this matter, Kurgan evokes the 'mass disappearance and reappearance of people in the city'.

Between resolutely top-down maps and those that position themselves on the personal level of individuals, there is a wealth of websites on which mapping tools are put to participatory use. One example that falls within this category is the French platform Carticipe, which was initially trialled in 2013 in Laval, western France, before being put into action in Strasbourg and then Marseilles: it enables residents to make online suggestions for

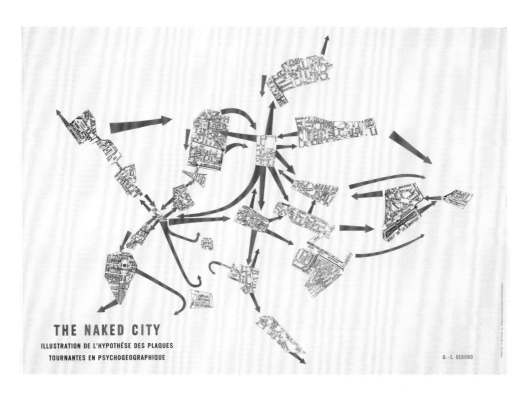

THE NAKED CITY

ILLUSTRATION DE L'HYPOTHÈSE DES PLAQUES
TOURNANTES EN PSYCHOGÉOGRAPHIQUE

G.-E. DEBORD

**Guy Debord and Asger Jorn, 'The Naked City', 1957**
This map illustrates the Situationists' approach to the city, or 'psychogeography'. According to its authors, the arrows represent slopes that link different 'unities of ambience' in Paris. They correspond to the natural tendencies of urban subjects to drift from one place to another. Blurring the distinction between subjective and objective, this reading of the city fosters a new understanding of its structure.

improvements to their city.[38] A large number of applications along these lines are in operation all over the world and allow citizens' ideas and opinions to be collected.

Urban mapping thus embraces the various gradations that lead from the neocybernetics-inspired city to its collaborative counterpart. In a whole series of cases, it even constitutes a meeting point of top-down and bottom-up. In the context of local life, one of its roles consists for example in making the structures of the city more readable so as to facilitate exchanges between municipal authorities and citizens. It is with this in view that cities such as Rennes, in western France, have launched projects to represent their territory in three dimensions.[39] However, we still need to remain conscious of the somewhat artificial character of this legibility. It relies on digital mapping's capacity to bring ever more diverse types of data together. Their heterogeneity is counterbalanced by their integration into interactive views. Members of the general public do not always fully understand the complexity of the multiple layers of information that allow streets, squares, infrastructure

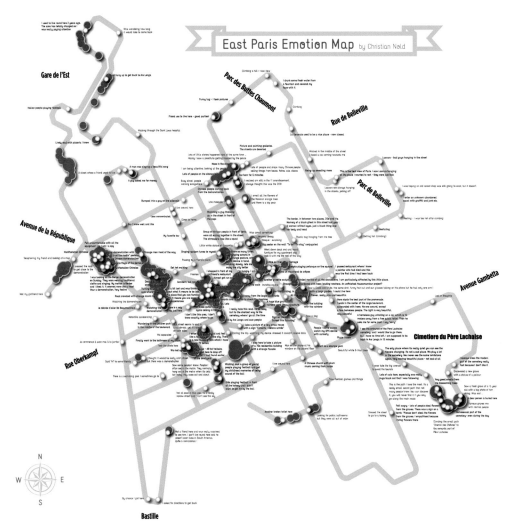

# East Paris Emotion Map, April 2008

The East Paris Emotion Map is the result of a two day intensive workshop by Christian Nold with 18 local people commissioned by Gallery Ars Longa. The participants explored the area around the 11th arrondissement whilst equipped with the special Bio Mapping tool invented by the artist. The device measured the participants' emotional arousal in relation to their geographical location in the city. On their return from the walk all the participants viewed their maps and guided by the artist analysed and annotated their own arousal data. On the map, the walks are represented by blue lines tracing the paths that people walked. The areas of high emotional arousal are represented by

red clusters. Arousal is not necessarily positive or negative and is best thought about in terms of heightened attention to one's body or surroundings. The white dots indicate where the participants added textual annotations to describe the variety of events and sensory stimuli that caused their emotional reactions during their walks. On the map we see an area of Paris on a Saturday and Sunday afternoon in April 2008. We see a mixture of people, events and places and the complex ways these are interwoven with each other. The general ambience is one of calmness but there are a few clearly defined annotation and high arousal clusters. The Situationists from the

1950s referred to them as 'unities of atmosphere'. While they thought of these unities as creating a fractured city of contrasting ambiences, this particular map of Paris presents a continuous 'event space' of flowing interactions. Right in the centre of the map, the main arousal cluster near the Parmentier Metro Station, is the place where the participants set off from and had to wait to connect to the satellites. On the Place de la République is a prominent arousal cluster caused by a Chinese, pro-Olympics demonstration on the Saturday and a Berber demonstration on Sunday in the same location. The cemetery in the east is a particular high arousal area as well as the busy

shopping area on Rue du Faubourg du Temple. Apart from these we see a huge diversity of spatially distributed events from stolen kisses, football games, surprise encounters with friends, 'lascars' and beautiful views of the city.

### Artwork and Design
Christian Nold 2008

Go to the website for the full quality PDF and raw data files:
www.paris.emotionmap.net

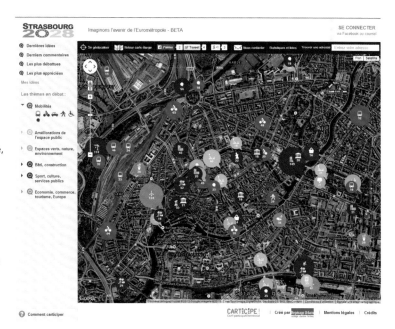

Screenshot of the 'Strasbourg 2028' website, 2015
Based on the Carticipe platform, 'Strasbourg 2028' enables inhabitants to post on the map suggestions to improve their city. The dark blue dots regard mobility improvements, the light blue ones public space improvements, the red ones buildings, the purple ones sports and culture, and finally the orange ones are related to the economy, commerce and tourism.

Christian Nold, 'East Paris Emotion Map', April 2008
Claiming the heritage of Situationist urbanism, Christian Nold produced this map of the north-east of Paris by equipping 18 local people with a special 'bio mapping tool' of his invention, which measured their degree of emotional arousal along a series of itineraries. The map aims to reveal a new geography of the city combining its physical organisation with the emotional load attached to certain places.

and parks to be visualised in order to 'federate, simulate and imagine the city of tomorrow', as a presentation brochure for Dassault Systèmes' 3DEXPERIENCity platform announces.[40]

Beyond the integration of heterogeneous data, the map appears as an interface that ensures consistency between the physical and digital worlds. By the same token, it plays a decisive role in the development of augmented reality. And since the city is ever more closely related to augmented reality, maps can sometimes seem to become confused with the urban organisms to which they refer. Another way of describing this convergence would be by noting that, while digital content initially offered liberation from city topography, the latter is more and more frequently providing the basis that allows us to find our bearings within a plethora of electronic realms. While the map represents the city, the city serves as a map. This coming together has inspired numerous research and development projects all around the world. In France, for instance, there was Terra Numerica, within the competitive cluster Cap Digital, which intended to work towards combining the physical organisation of cities with digital content from 3D modelling of urban spaces.[41] This sort of combination explains why authors who are investigating the future of urban mapping so often like to refer to the famous

short text 'Del rigor en la ciencia' ('On Exactitude in Science', 1946) in which Jorge Luis Borges, writing under the pseudonym of a fictional 17th-century character, conjured up a map of the Empire 'whose size was that of the Empire, and which coincided point for point with it', or to the slightly less well-known passage from Lewis Carroll's *Sylvie and Bruno Concluded* (1893) in which the country itself is used 'as its own map'.[42] The bridges between the city and the map, the latter understood in its broad sense that includes both 2D visualisations and surveillance, have become so numerous that it is tempting to amalgamate the two.

It is perhaps closer to reality to interpret their relationship along the lines of that between the body and its mental representations – representations which the Portuguese-American neurologist Antonio Damasio moreover calls 'maps'. Contrary to most traditional maps, notes Damasio, those that are produced by the brain are inseparable from the body that they chart. Above all, they possess the capacity to influence it permanently.[43] The inseparability between the city and digital maps may well turn out to be of the same type. Without the city, there are no maps; but the new maps of the city possess the power to change it, often in real time.

Behind this seductive analogy, new urban mapping can be interpreted in various ways. It can be considered as an infrastructure, in the sense

3D model presenting the draft new district of Maurepas Gayeulles. 3D data city of Rennes. 3D software component by Dassault Systèmes, 2015 Coupled with 3D visualisation, digital urban cartography enables municipal authorities to better present projects to their citizens. In France, the city of Rennes, in Brittany, has been a pioneer of this use of maps.

in which, like GPS technology, it ever more frequently constitutes the foundations on which regulation of the large-scale technological systems rests. It also appears as a tool allowing causes to be promoted, and information, sensations and even emotions to be shared. The map as a repository of experience is superimposed on the map as infrastructure; the map as an expression of a certain form of liberty confronts the map as an instrument of control.

At this stage, it is worth asking ourselves whether mapping in the digital era still ought to be understood in terms of representation of a reality that is external to it, or whether instead it constitutes a navigation device that allows trajectories to be defined and followed within this complex environment, inseparably technological and human, physical and electronic, that is the city. Such is the position argued by Valérie November, Eduardo Camacho-Hübner and Bruno Latour in a provocative article published in 2010 which places the emphasis on the performative dimension of maps.[44] This performative quality naturally points towards the evolution that is leading cities to become more and more muddled together with what happens within them.

While the strengthening of the performative dimension is undeniable, maps still continue to refer to our image of reality. In this sense, it is possible to say that they still represent reality itself. Similarly to the representations that our brains produce of the external environment, which in Damasio's terms constitute a different type of map than those that chart our bodies, they still mix up external data with interpretations and intentions. Maps never appear as pure representations, even if only in the sense that they partially reconstruct the elements that they seek to feature.[45]

If it seems important at this stage to retain this imaging function, it is because it appears to be one of the fundamental capacities of maps to make an active contribution to the constituent narratives of contemporary urbanism. Although these narratives are often substituted with urban plans, they still have just as much recourse to mapping, which appears as a guarantee that they are serious and, above all, self-fulfilling. *Real Time Rome*, for example, promises the advent of a city where it would be possible to continuously switch from tasks of general regulation to the monitoring of individual behaviours, much as the online retailer Amazon manages its clientele. As for OpenStreetMap's base maps, they announce the emergence of an urbanism founded on a large-scale collaborative approach.

Maps are not the same as plans. While the latters' capacity to anticipate would seem to have been exhausted, the map remains rich with all manner of possibilities. It is produced and read at the junction between humans and large-scale technological devices, or between group ventures and one-person businesses. It plays a central role in the emergence of a cyborg urbanism, in the construction of participatory communities, and in the pulsation that sees not just individuals but also cities of the digital era dispersing, then gathering themselves together, before dispersing again. More specifically, within these various processes, the production and use of maps can be assimilated into a sort of dawning of consciousness among stakeholders as to the challenges of their approach. The narrative dimension plays a part in this dawning of consciousness. The map tells the city's story to those who make it, and by the same token helps to give it a self-reflexive dimension. It is as though mapping were the medium through which the smart city attained a sort of self-consciousness, through all those who contribute to its development. The map allows the spatialised intelligence of the city to represent itself to itself.

Another way to perceive its role involves resorting to a monadical model in which each urban stakeholder contains the city in its entirety, but understood from a certain point of view. Models inspired by the theory

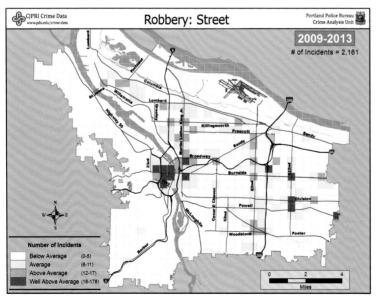

Criminal Justice Policy Research Institute, Portland University, map showing the spatial distribution of street robberies in Portland, Oregon, between 2009 and 2013
Displaying sensitive information, crime maps are inherently political. They constitute key instruments in many contemporary assessments of the problems that plague cities. They often have a direct impact on real estate values.

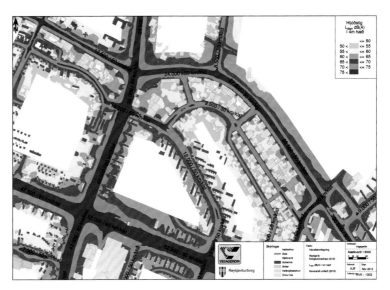

**Noise map of Reykjavik, Iceland, produced by the Environment Agency of Iceland, 2014**
Equally politically sensitive is the information displayed on noise maps. In many cities, their publication has been delayed for political reasons.

of monadology developed by Leibniz in the early 18th century and the interpretation of it that Gilles Deleuze offers in *The Fold: Leibniz and the Baroque* (first published in French in 1988) have been popular over the last few years among digital theorists.[46] Indeed, they provide an elegant solution to the question of how individuals can reveal themselves to be both inseparable from their physical and electronic environment and distinct from one another. If this sort of framework is adopted, mapping acts as an expression of these different viewpoints as well as of the dynamics that their coexistence entails. The intelligence of the city can also be imagined as the outcome of these perspectives.

Behind this sort of speculation, maps crystallise a series of crucial issues. They allow groups to come together. Today, city politics is decided ever more frequently through maps and through the narratives of which they form one of the preferred media, and this at the same time as the traditional plan has seen a certain fall from favour, as has already been mentioned. Above all, maps participate in the construction of what is made visible to all: a process that is eminently political, no doubt. Certain individuals are invested with the power to decide which data will be selected, as well as the way in which they will be clustered together in order to be revealed to others. Not everyone has the right to see everything. Some cartographic constructions are highly sensitive, such as the British and

American crime maps that directly influence property prices, or the maps of noise and pollution on which so many European municipal authorities struggle to communicate.[47]

On this subject, it is hard not to be reminded of Jacques Rancière's incisive analyses (referred to in the Introduction) of the links between politics and aesthetics through what he calls 'the distribution of the sensible': that is, the way in which what is made visible reveals both the existence of things in common and subdivisions that stipulate each individual's place and prerogatives within the overall social and political structure.[48] In this broader sense, the map is revealed to be inseparably political and aesthetic.[49]

## A New Aesthetic

Mapping provides a useful reminder of the importance of aesthetic factors in the rise of the smart city. From this point of view, the transfiguration of urban fabric mentioned above is not unlike the one that electricity brought about in its time. Indeed, electricity created favourable conditions for the emergence of a new aesthetic sensibility based on new atmospheres and rhythms. A similar phenomenon seems to be emerging today. The prominence of aesthetics allows a better understanding of the role played by artists, designers and architects, alongside novelists and scriptwriters, in exploring the smart city. It allows quite different phenomena to be linked together, such as the cartographic dimension that is present in so many artists' projects and the ornamental impulse that is typical of digital architecture.

Such connections are based on the spread of techniques and effects such as pixelation and the use of patterns. Pixelation in particular is one of the signs of this 'new aesthetic' that is impregnated with digital culture, of which the British artist and writer James Bridle has made himself the messenger.[50] But instead of reserving this term for art and design, it is perhaps more interesting to make it one of the characteristics of a new urban sensibility that is expressed on different levels, from street furniture to the atmosphere of streets and cafés, and from city maps freely reinterpreted by artists to the interior decor of buildings. Besides the obsessive references to pixels or infinitely repeatable patterns, this new aesthetic is nourished by a whole series of other techniques and effects. As if to express the troubling poetics of augmented reality, it favours a piling up of layers and effects of transparency that allow the overlapping content to be read. Of course, the use of Photoshop is not foreign to this infatuation. This aesthetic often involves a blurring of scales and a dizziness that stem from the possibility of continuously zooming in and out: a possibility that was exploited by the American designers Charles and Ray Eames in their 1977 documentary *Powers of Ten* and which has become commonplace in applications such as Google Earth. It thrives on the mingling of different types of sensory impressions. Sight, touch and taste thus forge unlikely alliances with fields from architecture to the culinary arts to fashion. The mingling of sight and touch in particular constitutes one of the fundamental motivations of contemporary architectural ornamentation.

Ultimately, this aesthetic relates to the fundamental pulsation of the individual in the digital era, between dispersal and refocusing. By embodying this rhythmic alternation, augmented reality and geolocation succeed in revealing their complementarity, as we have seen. Both the cartographic and the ornamental dimensions of contemporary urban aesthetics are also concerned with it. Ornament and maps relate both to the many links and the continuum between contemporary subjects and the world around them, and the possibility for the same subjects to become deliberately detached from this continuum by affirming their localised presence and their unique capacity to experience pleasure.

Keiichi Matsuda, 'Augmented (hyper) Reality' production drawing, 2009
London-based designer Keiichi Matsuda's explorations of the perspective opened by augmented reality involve a series of aesthetic effects including the blurring of the distinction between 2D and 3D representations, transparencies and superimpositions.

# Laboratories of Public Life in the Digital Age

The age we are living in has witnessed the emergence of two types of area where the information society in its mature state is more clearly defined than it is elsewhere. The first of these areas is higher education. With the development of online learning, the question of the importance that physical space is likely to retain in the construction of collective experiences and meaning is posed particularly clearly. Beyond learning per se, one of the missions of universities is to develop shared references and meanings. Traditionally, the fact of students and professors rubbing shoulders in lecture halls and classrooms made a powerful contribution to this process of construction. So where do things stand in the era of massive open online courses (MOOCs)?[51] While the importance of many university spaces is in decline – do we still need grand lecture halls, now that there is the option of online learning? – others, such as libraries and residential facilities for students, are seeing their roles transformed or even intensified. A new geography of higher education, symbolic of certain key issues of society in the digital era, is starting to emerge.

The second of these laboratories is the city. As in the case of higher education, the question is posed as to how to build collective experiences and meanings within societies that accord an ever greater importance to individuals who are often glued to their computer screens or smartphones. The political dimension of this question is even clearer in relation to the urban realm. Elected officials have made no mistake about it, and working groups, task forces, committees and commissions charged with defining strategies that are tailored to the challenges presented are springing up all over the place. The strategies are fairly wide-ranging: resolutely technological in Singapore; more oriented towards citizen participation in Paris; extremely ambitious, at least on paper, in the cases of metropolises such as London and Vienna; more limited for cities like Accra and Valparaíso. However, they all have one thing in common, which could well appear with hindsight to be the main illusion of the beginnings of the digital era: that of a city whose workings would be not fundamentally changed, but simply improved by a massive injection of digital technology.

It is an illusion, because to imagine that conditions of public life and mechanisms of political representation and decision-making could essentially remain preserved in the configuration they had before the rise of information and communications technology is more a matter of wishful thinking than it is a realistic scenario. The moving of collective deliberations and debates to the online realm has gone hand in hand with a shift in collective practices that cannot be ignored. As mentioned in the previous chapter, people rarely vote online, and well-organised opinion groups can acquire a level of influence that extends well beyond the sectors of the population they truly represent. Winning large-scale online debates often comes down to ramping up the pressure under terms that are more reminiscent of viral propagation than of seeking majority approval within clearly defined boundaries.[52] Of course, these sorts of distortions already existed in traditional democratic processes, but they are magnified by the partial autonomy of electronic avatars in comparison with flesh-and-blood human beings. Added to this is the prospect of conversations that introduce non-human participants which will soon be endowed with intelligence, to varying degrees and in different fields, from digital infrastructure to programs intended to moderate humans' collaborative enterprises. We will need to learn to deliberate in the company of algorithms that will increasingly have their own say on how things develop. Even if artificial intelligence may not necessarily threaten the existence of the human species as Stephen Hawking fears (see chapter 2), if only because of the competitive advantage that our bodies give us within an extended range of possibilities, its very existence will change the nature of politics. The dramatic arrival of the question of animal rights in public debate, like in France where a law was recently passed to recognise animals as 'living, sentient beings' that deserve to be treated as such, may represent an unconscious way of preparing ourselves for what still seems to be a leap into the unknown, as if it were time for humans to acknowledge the rights of those other than themselves – perhaps animals will be followed by intelligent algorithms – before welcoming them to the negotiation table.

Mapping can offer a different model for collective decision-making. Contributing alongside others to the creation of a map, referring to it and using it to find our way around, always in relation to people other than ourselves: all of these seemingly banal actions are instrumental to the organisation of the city in real time. They can be compared to standpoints within a new type of public space that is both physical and digital, where initiatives are not the work of humans alone, but where humans still retain the privilege of defining the values that guide them. There is no collective intelligence without shared values, or without a code of ethics that stipulates what is desirable and what is not. In addition to being laboratories of public life in the digital era, smart cities are also destined to become the melting pot of a new collective morality.

# References

1 See for instance Antonio Damasio, *Self Comes to Mind: Constructing the Conscious Brain*, Pantheon Books (New York), 2010.

2 Andy Crabtree and Tom Rodden, 'Hybrid Ecologies: Understanding Cooperative Interaction in Emerging Physical-Digital Environments', *Personal and Ubiquitous Computing*, vol 12, no 7, 2008, pp 481–93. For a more general take on the notion of digital augmentation, see Jean Daniélou and François Ménard, *L'Art d'augmenter les villes (pour) une enquête sur la ville intelligente*, Plan Urbanisme Construction Architecture (Paris), 2013.

3 'Urbanflow Helsinki', http://helsinki.urbanflow.io/ (consulted 10 February 2015); 'LinkNYC', http://www.link.nyc/ (consulted 10 February 2015).

4 'Cluny numérique', http://cluny-numerique.fr/index.php (consulted 10 February 2015).

5 Nicolas Nova, *Les Médias géolocalisés: Comprendre les nouveaux médias numériques*, FYP éditions (Limoges), 2009; Eric Gordon and Adriana de Souza e Silva, *Net Locality: Why Location Matters in a Networked World*, Wiley-Blackwell (Chichester), 2011.

6 'Laura Kurgan: You Are Here', http://www.macba.cat/en/exhibition-laura-kurgan/1/exhibition-archive/expo (consulted 16 February 2015).

7 'The Drawing of my Life', http://www.planbperformance.net/index.php?id=danmapping (consulted 16 February 2015).

8 See Gilles Deleuze, *The Fold: Leibniz and the Baroque* [*Le Pli: Leibniz et le baroque*, 1988], English translation, University of Minnesota Press (Minneapolis), 1993.

9 William J Mitchell, *City of Bits: Space, Place, and the Infobahn*, MIT Press (Cambridge, Massachusetts), 1995.

10 See for instance Joel Kotkin, *The New Geography: How the Digital Revolution is Reshaping the American Landscape* [2000], new edition, Random House (New York), 2001.

11 Serge Wachter, *La Ville interactive: L'Architecture et l'urbanisme au risque du numérique et de l'écologie*, L'Harmattan (Paris), 2010.

12 On these new architectural geometries, see Antoine Picon, *Digital Culture in Architecture: An Introduction for the Design Professions*, Birkhäuser (Basel), 2010.

13 http://sol-logic.com/etree/ (consulted 16 February 2015).

14 http://www.22barcelona.com/ (consulted 17 February 2015); http://www.songdo.com/ (consulted 17 February 2015); http://www.songdo.com/songdo-international-business-district/why-songdo/a-brand-new-city.aspx (consulted 17 February 2015).

15 See Antoine Picon, *Claude Perrault 1613–1688 ou la curiosité d'un classique*, Picard (Paris), 1988.

16 On the megastructural movement, see Reyner Banham, *Megastructure: Urban Futures of the Recent Past*, Thames & Hudson (London), 1976. On New Urbanism, see for instance Tigran Haas, *New Urbanism and Beyond: Designing Cities for the Future*, Rizzoli (New York), 2008.

17 On the architectural relevance of stacking today, see Preston Scott Cohen, 'Successive Architecture', *Log*, no 32, 2014, pp 153–63.

18 Eva Herrmann, '666 Meters, 888 Meters or rather 1,111

Meters?', *Mapolis*, 4 June 2011, http://architecture. mapolismagazin.com/jds-architects-shenzhen-logistics-center-shenzhen (consulted 8 February 2015); Paolo Soleri, *Arcology: The City in the Image of Man*, MIT Press (Cambridge, Massachusetts), 1969.

**19** Dominique Lorrain, 'Les Industriels japonais de l'environnement', *Flux*, no 50, October–December 2002, pp 80–90.

**20** See on this type of project Mohsen Mostafavi and Gareth Doherty (eds), *Ecological Urbanism*, Harvard Graduate School of Design (Cambridge, Massachusetts) and Lars Müller (Baden, Switzerland), 2010.

**21** Olivier Coutard, 'Services urbains: La Fin des grands réseaux?', in Olivier Coutard and Jean-Pierre Lévy (eds), *Ecologies urbaines*, Economica (Paris), 2010, pp 102–29.

**22** http://www.bridj.com/ (consulted 9 February 2015); on this subject, see also Katharine Q Seelye, 'To Lure Bostonians, New "Pop-Up" Bus Service Learns Riders' Rhythms', *New York Times*, 4 June 2014, http://www. nytimes.com/2014/06/05/us/ to-lure-bostonians-new-pop-up-bus-service-learns-riders-rhythms.html (consulted 9 February 2015).

**23** Stephen Graham and Simon Marvin, *Splintering Urbanism: Networked Infrastructures, Technological Mobilities and the Urban Condition*, Routledge (London and New York), 2001.

**24** See Khaldoun Zreik (ed), *Nouvelles cartographies, nouvelles villes: HyperUrbain.2*, Europia (Paris), 2010, as well as *Les Cahiers de l'Institut d'aménagement et d'urbanisme*, no 166, October 2013.

**25** On this shift, see for instance Jean-François Coulais, *Images virtuelles et horizons du regard: Visibilités calculées dans l'histoire des représentations*, MetisPresses (Geneva), 2014.

**26** 'Websites using Google Maps', http://trends.builtwith. com/websitelist/Google-Maps (consulted 17 February 2015).

**27** Patrice Flichy, *Le Sacre de l'amateur: Sociologie des passions ordinaires à l'ère numèrique*, Le Seuil (Paris), 2010.

**28** Bruno Latour and Émilie Hermant, *Paris ville invisible*, Les Empêcheurs de Penser en Rond and La Découverte (Paris), 1998.

**29** 'Real Time Rome', http://senseable.mit.edu/ realtimerome/ (consulted 17 February 2015).

**30** 'New York Talk Exchange', http://senseable.mit.edu/ nyte/ (consulted 17 February 2015). See also Francisca M Rojas, Clelia Caldesi Valeri, Kristian Kloeckl and Carlo Ratti (eds), *NYTE: New York Talk Exchange*, SA+P Press (Cambridge, Massachusetts), 2008.

**31** Interestingly, events such as the Fête de la Musique in Paris and the final of the European football championship in Madrid in 2008 have also been the focus of Urban Mobs. 'Urban Mobs', http://www. urbanmobs.fr/en/ (consulted 17 February 2015).

**32** http://www.cityzenith.com/ (consulted 17 February 2015).

**33** http://www.synthicity.com/ (consulted 17 February 2015).

**34** http://www. appliedautonomy.com/isee. html (consulted 17 February 2015).

**35** 'Architecture and Justice,

Million Dollar Blocks', http://
spatialinformationdesignlab.
org/projects/million-dollar-
blocks (consulted 17 February
2015).
**36** Simon Sadler, *The
Situationist City*, MIT Press
(Cambridge, Massachusetts),
1998; Antoine Picon and Jean-
Paul Robert, *Un Atlas parisien:
Le dessus des cartes*, Editions
du Pavillon de l'Arsenal, Picard
(Paris), 1999.
**37** http://www.christiannold.
com/ (consulted 17
February 2015). See also the
contributions to the catalogue
of the exhibition organised in
2003 by the Palais de Tokyo in
Paris: *GNS, Global Navigation
System*, Editions Cercle d'Art
(Paris), 2003.
**38** 'Carticipe! Outil participatif
territorial', http://carticipe.net/
(consulted 17 February 2015).
**39** 'RM3D', http://www.
metropole3d.rennes.fr/
(consulted 17 February 2015).
**40** 'Fédérer, simuler et prédire
la ville de demain': Dassault
Systèmes, *La Plateforme
3DEXPERIENCity*, commercial
brochure (2013).
**41** 'Terra Numerica: La
Numérisation du patrimoine
urbain', http://competitivite.
gouv.fr/projets-en-fin-de-
conventionnement-fui/

fiche-projet-abouti-576/terra-
numerica-2.
html?cHash=4908e59c-
58f5e66e6ea44d6fab34870e
(consulted 17 February 2015).
**42** For instance Gilles Palsky,
'Borges, Carroll et la carte
au 1/1', *Cybergeo: European
Journal of Geography*,
September 1999, http://
cybergeo.revues.org/5233
(consulted 17 February 2015).
**43** Damasio 2010.
**44** Valérie November,
Eduardo Camacho-Hübner
and Bruno Latour, 'Entering
a Risky Territory: Space in the
Age of Digital Navigation',
*Environment and Planning D:
Society and Space*, vol 28,
no 4, 2010, pp 581–99.
**45** See Denis Cosgrove,
*Mappings*, Reaktion Books
(London), 1999.
**46** Gottfried Wilhelm Freiherr
von Leibniz, *Discourse on
Metaphysics; and, The
Monadology* [*Discours de
métaphysique*, 1686 and *La
Monadologie*, 1714], English
translation, Prometheus Books
(Buffalo, New York), 1992;
Deleuze [1988] 1993; see also
Picon 2013.
**47** On noise maps, see
for instance Olivier Balaÿ,
'Cartes à l'écoute de la
ville: Prolégomènes pour

le renouvellement des
cartographies acoustiques de la
ville européenne', in Khaldoun
Zreik (ed) 2013, pp 81–92.
**48** Jacques Rancière, *The
Politics of Aesthetics* [*Le
Partage du sensible: Esthétique
et politique*, 2000], translated
by Gabriel Rockhill, Continuum
(London and New York), 2004,
p 12.
**49** On this question, see Laura
Kurgan, *Close Up at a Distance:
Mapping, Technology, and
Politics*, Zone Books (New
York), 2013.
**50** James Bridle, 'The New
Aesthetic: Waving at the
Machines', 5 December
2011, http://booktwo.org/
notebook/waving-at-machines/
(consulted 17 February 2015).
See also Bruce Sterling, 'An
Essay on the New Aesthetic',
*Wired*, 2 April 2012, http://
www.wired.com/2012/04/an-
essay-on-the-new-aesthetic/
(consulted 17 February 2015).
**51** On the spectacular
development of MOOCs, see
for instance Paul Kim (ed),
*Massive Open Online Courses:
The MOOC Revolution*,
Routledge (New York), 2014.
**52** See Dominique Cardon,
*La Démocratie Internet:
Promesses et limites*, Le Seuil
(Paris), 2010.

# Conclusion
## The Challenges of Intelligence

As we have seen, the smart city, being both an ideal and a process – a dual aspect that allows it to escape the language of mere urban utopias – remains full of ambiguities. It also faces a certain number of challenges that are simultaneously technological, environmental, social and cultural, and which demand to be discussed as we approach the end of this book. It is not that any of them represents an insurmountable obstacle or an asymptotic limit that cannot be crossed. Rather, they can be considered as an incitement to enrich current approaches. In particular, we need to leave in the past what is still the overly simplified quality of representations of the smart city proposed by the various stakeholders that it concerns. We cannot satisfy ourselves with one or two models of the smart city. The head-on conflict between neocybernetics-inspired management and participatory logic should not lead us to limit the range of possibilities. Instead, it is a question of extending this range in order to reveal the existence of alternatives, taking local situations into account as well as the targets that leaders and the general public set themselves.

## The Limits of All-Digital Solutions

As is the case with all positive interpretations, that of the smart city leaves aside a whole set of troubling realities, starting with the emerging tensions between the intensive use of information and communications technology and the need for sustainable development. Is digital technology really as 'green' as its stalwart supporters claim? It is worth reminding ourselves that it is not merely an ethereal presence, but exists materially; and that the smart city's servers, cables and aerials, without even mentioning its millions of chips and sensors, have a heavy impact on the environment.[1] Servers give off heat, while cables, circuit boards and discarded screens bring up sensitive issues in

**The CERN Data Centre, near Geneva, 2008** Contrary to what expressions like 'the cloud' suggest, digital resources possess a strong material side. The largest research facility in Europe, CERN was also the place where the World Wide Web was invented.

Ghanaians working in
Agbogbloshie, Ghana, 23
March 2011
A suburb of Accra,
Agbogbloshie is one of
the places where used
electronics end up. Waste
processing includes health-
damaging practices such as
burning.

relation to recycling, which is often subcontracted to developing countries
with barely a thought for the health of the people taking it on. Information
and communications technology already consumes almost 10 per cent of the
global electricity supply: that is, 50 per cent more energy than the entire air
transport industry.[2] The annual volume of electronic waste produced across
the planet was estimated at 41.5 million tonnes in 2011, and may well reach
93.5 million in 2016.[3]

These statistics do not call the ideal of the smart city into question; but
they do point towards a need for greater discernment in harnessing the
technologies on which it depends. Digital technology has both a financial
and an environmental cost. Consequently, its use needs to be modulated
in relation to the characteristics of the urban areas that it is set to serve.
To put it in the simplest terms, the greater the density of capital and
population, as is the case in the heart of major cities, the more investments

in information and communications technology can be justified, even if they risk exacerbating the imbalance between centres and suburbs – a subject to which we will return. A specific economy for the smart city is crucially needed.

This economy needs to be coupled with moral standards that are both collective and individual. Reviving a sort of behavioural restraint, they should go against the inducements to consume ever greater quantities of digital resources and equipment that the main stakeholders in the sector are constantly directing at the public. It is worth remembering that even carrying out a Google search on a mobile phone at a street corner consumes energy. Aside from broader questions such as those concerning the relationship between humans and machines that are invested with some sort of intelligence, the morality of the smart city should probably begin with more judicious use of smartphones.

Besides the environmental challenges, there are other pitfalls that threaten the viability of the smart city. Despite the ever more numerous surveillance cameras scrutinising its residents' and visitors' whereabouts and activities, the smart city is particularly vulnerable to vandalism and terrorism, which can quite easily disrupt the workings of its essential infrastructure. Added to threats in physical space is the prospect of cyber-attack. Cities made of atoms and data bits sometimes seem more fragile than their predecessors built of brick, stone and concrete.

But, at the same time, it is worth remembering that every new type of technology has its own specific forms of vulnerability. Electricity currently remains cities' principal source of weakness. It is no accident that so many futuristic novels depict its disappearance as a precursor to the apocalypse or to a return to barbarity. Living in a city means accepting its weaknesses, while constantly thinking of ways to mitigate its most disastrous effects. For example, where digital technology is concerned, it is advisable to establish ways of getting around the automated management of vital infrastructure in case of a major malfunction, whether accidental or criminal in origin. Think for example of the electric cars whose windows cannot be opened if their electrical system fails, or lifts that get stuck and hold their users prisoner during a power cut. With the onslaught of information and communications technology, this type of problem needs to be limited as much as possible. This is the price that has to be paid for city intelligence.

# The Necessary Diversification of Scenarios

Other challenges stem from the emphasis that most stakeholders place on the knowledge economy, to the detriment of more traditional manufacturing activities. This is the reason for the emblematic role played in much discourse by urban areas such as Silicon Valley and the region around Boston, Massachusetts, where universities and high-tech businesses requiring very highly educated individuals predominate. It sometimes seems as though industrial towns are not called to become intelligent, especially if they are situated in developing countries where the rights of individuals are still widely infringed. Besides, can the techniques of urban management that form the basis of the smart city be applied to situations of post-industrial decline? It is a noteworthy fact that Detroit rarely features among the examples cited in relation to the hypothesis of the smart city.

**Massachusetts Institute of Technology Campus, Cambridge, Massachusetts** Despite its appeal, the 'knowledge economy' epitomised by places such as Silicon Valley or Cambridge, Massachusetts cannot be the only model for imagining the development of smart cities.

I referred above to the need to introduce sorts of gradients, for example between the centre and the suburbs, when equipping cities with information and communications technology. Does this mean that the outskirts are called

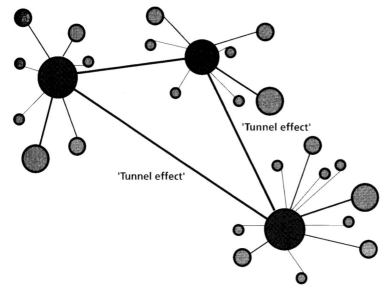

'Tunnel effect'

'Tunnel effect'

François Ascher, 'tunnel effects' between distant highly developed urban districts, from Stephen Graham and Simon Marvin (eds), *Splintering Urbanism*, Routledge (London and New York), 2001
Through communication infrastructures, distant urban districts, for instance the City of London and Wall Street in New York, may appear closer to one another than these districts are to their immediate surroundings. Such 'tunnel effects' challenge traditional modes of urban governance.

to become less intelligent than city centres? And what of the countryside? Is the smart city leading to a reinvention of the split between town and country that had been gradually called into question under the influence of factors such as the advent of modern media, chiefly radio and television?

On a more general level, questions might be asked about the political and social ideals to which most advocates of the smart city subscribe, whether implicitly or explicitly. In *Splintering Urbanism*, Stephen Graham and Simon Marvin hold digital technology responsible for an increasing series of ruptures: between hyperconnected neighbourhoods, in touch with the global economy and linked together by sorts of high-speed communication tunnels, and neglected urban areas; or between stakeholders in the global economy and residents relegated to menial tasks.[4] Graham and Marvin claim that the age of urban networks which served to integrate society has given way to an era in which technology shows itself to be incapable of curbing the most glaring differences. Worse, it has even exacerbated them.

In fact, these authors fail to recall that there was nothing egalitarian about the political project that underpinned the emergence of the networked city of the industrial era. Far from seeking to eradicate social differences, Paris in

B+H Architects, SmartCity
Kochi, Kochi, Kerala, India,
2015
Located at approximately
11 kilometres (7 miles)
from downtown Kochi, in
the Indian state of Kerala,
SmartCity Kochi is a special
economic zone oriented
towards the development
and use of information
technology. In addition to its
economic and technological
components, the project aims
to provide its inhabitants
with all the amenities of
modern urban life.

the age of Napoleon III and Baron Haussmann simply set out to make them tolerable by inserting middle-class districts and working-class suburbs in a single mesh that combined water and sanitation systems, a road network, pleasure gardens and parks such as the Buttes-Chaumont.[5] The Internet has merely appropriated this ideal of cohabitation, without reducing its inherent inequality. By the same token, narratives on the smart city are neither more nor less generous than the ones that presided over the setting up of the major urban networks of the industrial era.

Again, the problem has more to do with the failure to take the diversity of city functions into account, and with the impossibility of reducing this to a simple question of intelligence. Writers from Richard Florida to Edward Glaeser have arguably placed too much emphasis on the importance of the 'creative class', which is supposed to represent the brain of the smart city, and not enough on the role of its muscles: traditional services and industry.[6] Above all, there cannot be only one or two scenarios that lead to this city. Diversification is clearly necessary at this point, even if only because situations differ greatly from one country to another.

While India's decision to develop intelligent cities can only be applauded, it is still reasonable to ask questions on the country's strategy of imitating Western, Middle Eastern, Chinese and Korean models, without seeking to capitalise more on the inventiveness of an urban population that is accustomed to using smartphones, even in the slums of megalopolises such as New Delhi and Mumbai.[7] As expressions of 'impatient capital', to borrow the term coined by Rahul Mehrotra, which is causing a proliferation of glass office buildings and conference centres all over the planet, the Indian projects would certainly benefit from being linked up to the rich range of digital practices that are already present in the country's cities.[8]

The paths leading to the smart city cannot be the same in Europe, where cities possess a rich heritage of traditional infrastructure, from sanitation to public transport, as they are in the metropolises of developing countries where this infrastructure is often lacking. In the latter, the inadequacy of facilities is often offset by residents' resourcefulness: their ability

**Mobile phone use in India: Dharavi, Mumbai, 25 October 2011**
Smart cities in rapidly developing countries like India should build on the abilities of their youths. Even in slums, like here in Dharavi, the use of smartphones has become quite common.

to make do and mend through inventively blending technologies and devices, wheelbarrows and multimedia sound systems, or broken robots and interactive screens.[9] Without questioning the need for large cities in developing countries to be gradually provided with facilities, it is possible to imagine other ways to the smart city than through a proliferation of sensors intended better to control the functioning of heavy infrastructure. Once more, the scenarios need to be diversified, and well beyond what companies such as IBM and Cisco are proposing, just as the networked city of the industrial era took very different forms in Europe, the United States and Japan in the 19th and 20th centuries.

## Public/Private

'All that happens must be known'; 'Secrets are lies'; 'Privacy is theft': in *The Circle*, the American novelist Dave Eggers imagines a business based on Google and Facebook, where these sorts of slogans do the rounds.[10] There could be no better way of summarising the main ambiguities of the political and social discourse put forward by the advocates of a digital brave new world in which nothing would escape the notice of either the decision-makers or the public: a modern version of Bentham's Panopticon and Foucault's panopticism, in which the major part of the surveillance was carried out by the inmates themselves.[11] The smart city is not immune to this ambiguity, given that it seems to rely partially on individuals' acceptance of repeated intrusions into their private life. Even if these intrusions are accepted by large swathes of 'digital natives' – members of the generations that have grown up with the Internet – not all aspects of this evolution are beneficial.[12]

The increasing privatisation of entire areas of cities, which generally goes hand in hand with a reinforcement of surveillance, is a move in the same direction: a blurring or even a questioning of the dividing line between public and private. Does this mean that we should accept everything, for the sake of security, control and the need to share information? Here again, the solution may well lie in the emergence of new codes of ethics, undoubtedly quite different from the ones that governed the relationship between public and private in the past, but sufficiently prescriptive to preserve the essential aspect of the right to a private life and personal secrets (as long as they are neither 'lies' nor 'theft').

## From Event to History

Despite the challenges described here, the rise of the smart city constitutes a genuine revolution, comparable in significance to the birth of the major industrial cities in the 19th century and the emergence of the networked city as both an urban ideal and a physical process of city transformation. While this revolution's impact on urban form is still shrouded in uncertainty, its influence on the temporal structures of urban experience can already be observed. We live in cities that move to the rhythm of ever more numerous events which can be followed in real time.

But the proliferation of happenings goes hand in hand with a glaring absence of historical perspective, as if the possibility of history had been suspended indefinitely in favour of an eternal present or a future so close to what we already know that it seems to be a mere intensification of current conditions. The environmental apocalypse still remains the only notable prospect of change.

**The Las Vegas Strip at night, 2012**
A place emblematic of our contemporary urban condition. On the Strip, something is constantly happening, but the overall impression is that of an everlasting present.

**Aldo Rossi, 'La Città Analoga' (The Analogous City), 1976**
With this famous collage, the Italian architect Aldo Rossi (1931–1997) reminds us that history and collective memory, composition and superimposition, harmony and conflict are constitutive of the city as we know it. The city appears as a palimpsest of interventions of all kinds. Smart cities cannot be conceived all at once; they must allow for similar processes of accretion.

Of course, digital technology plays a key role in this impression. Indeed, the Internet is the most obvious embodiment of this world of events without clear historical pointers, that we often find ourselves thrust into. In this respect it remains faithful to the original metaphor of cyberspace, like the sort of giant Las Vegas Strip proposed by authors such as William Gibson in *Neuromancer*.[13] In Las Vegas, there is always something going on. Spectacular and saturated with clashing signs, atmospheres and colours, the giant hotels – from Caesars Palace to the Venetian, and from the New York-New York to the Paris – appear as events in themselves. But nothing ever seems to change, and the feverish activity of tourists and personnel alike generates nothing other than its own repetition. Facebook and Twitter give a fairly similar impression of hyperactivity and repetition. This in turn is communicated to cities, which we willingly see as set in a state of eternal youth, with

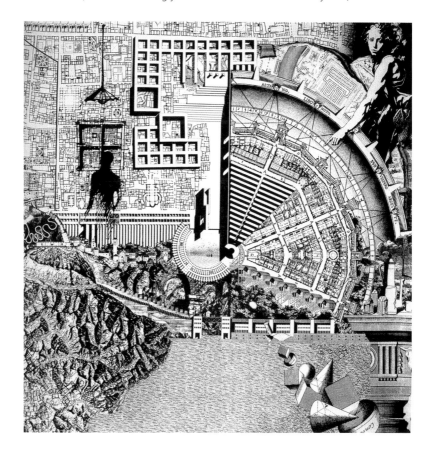

electronic exchanges playing the role of regenerating fluid. The era when the city appeared as a palimpsest of interventions recalling the role of history seems to be over. And yet the world still marches on, and social and political change looms on the horizon of an enlightened dream which is sometimes reminiscent of the 'spectacle' that Guy Debord tirelessly denounced.[14] How can we escape from this both enchanted and vicious circle? How can smart cities be made to age? This last challenge is closely linked to the need for a diversification of the models that guide these cities' development. It is a challenge that urgently needs to be met. That is the price to be paid for the future: a different future, rich in promise.

# References

**1** See Andrew Blum, *Tubes: A Journey to the Center of the Internet*, HarperCollins (New York), 2012.
**2** Mark P Mills, *The Cloud Begins with Coal: Big Data, Big Networks, Big Infrastructure, and Big Power. An Overview of the Electricity Used by the Global Digital Ecosystem*, research report for the National Mining Association and the American Coalition for Clean Coal Electricity, August 2013, http://www.tech-pundit.com/wp-content/uploads/2013/07/Cloud_Begins_With_Coal.pdf?c761ac (consulted 19 February 2015).
**3** 'E-Waste to Exceed 93.5 Million Tons Annually', *Environmental Leader*, 24 February 2014, http://www.environmentalleader.com/2014/02/24/e-waste-to-exceed-93-5-million-tons-annually/ (consulted 21 February 2015).
**4** Stephen Graham and Simon Marvin, *Splintering Urbanism: Networked Infrastructures, Technological Mobilities and the Urban Condition*, Routledge (London and New York), 2001.
**5** Antoine Picon, *La Ville des réseaux: Un imaginaire politique*, Editions Manucius (Paris), 2014.
**6** Richard Florida, *The Rise of the Creative Class: And How It's Transforming Work, Leisure, Community, and Everyday Life*, Basic Books (New York), 2002; Edward Glaeser, *Triumph of the City: How Our Greatest Invention Makes Us Richer, Smarter, Greener, Healthier, and Happier*, Penguin Press (New York), 2011.
**7** Uma Vishnu, '34% in Slums Have No Toilet, but 63% Own Mobile Phone in India', *Indian Express*, 22 March 2013, http://archive.indianexpress.com/news/34--in-slums-have-no-toilet-but-63--own-mobile-phone/1091573/ (consulted 21 February 2015).
**8** Rahul Mehrotra, *Architecture in India since 1990*, Pictor Publishing (Mumbai), 2011.
**9** See Nicolas Nova, *Futurs? La Panne des imaginaires technologiques*, Les Moutons Electriques (Montélimar), 2014, p 72, and above all Adam Greenfield, 'The Smartest Cities Rely on Citizen Cunning and Unglamorous Technology', *The Guardian*, 22 December 2014, http://www.theguardian.com/cities/2014/dec/22/the-smartest-cities-rely-on-citizen-cunning-and-unglamorous-technology (consulted 21 February 2015).
**10** Dave Eggers, *The Circle*, McSweeney's Books (San Francisco), 2013.
**11** See Michel Foucault, *Discipline and Punish: The Birth of the Prison [Surveiller et punir: Naissance de la prison*, 1975], English translation, Vintage Books (New York), 1995.
**12** John Palfrey and Urs Gasser, *Born Digital: Understanding the First Generation of Digital Natives*, Basic Books (New York), 2008.
**13** William Gibson, *Neuromancer*, Ace Books (New York), 1984.
**14** Guy Debord, *The Society of the Spectacle [La Société du spectacle*, 1967], English translation, Zone Books (New York), 1994.

# Bibliography

Batty, Michael, *The New Science of Cities*, MIT Press (Cambridge, Massachusetts), 2013

Cardon, Dominique, *La Démocratie Internet: Promesses et limites*, Le Seuil (Paris), 2010

Châtelet, Valérie (ed), *Anomalie Digital Arts*, no 6, 'Interactive Cities', HYX (Orléans), February 2007

Coutard, Olivier, 'Services urbains: La Fin des grands réseaux?', in Olivier Coutard and Jean-Pierre Lévy (eds), *Ecologies urbaines*, Economica (Paris), 2010, pp 102–29

Coutard, Olivier, Hanley, Richard and Zimmerman, Rae (eds), *Sustaining Urban Networks: The Social Diffusion of Large Technical Systems*, Routledge (London), 2004

Damasio, Antonio, *Self Comes to Mind: Constructing the Conscious Brain*, Pantheon Books (New York), 2010

Dehaene, Stanislas, *Consciousness and the Brain: Deciphering How the Brain Codes Our Thoughts*, Viking (New York), 2014

Dupuy, Gabriel and Tarr, Joel (eds), *Technology and the Rise of the Networked City in Europe and America*, Temple University Press (Philadelphia), 1988

Edwards, Paul, *The Closed World: Computers and the Politics of Discourse in Cold War America*, MIT Press (Cambridge, Massachusetts), 1996

Eychenne, Fabien, *La Ville 2.0, complexe … et familière*, FYP Éditions (Limoges), 2008

Flichy, Patrice, *Le Sacre de l'amateur: Sociologie des passions ordinaires à l'ère numérique*, Le Seuil (Paris), 2010

Florida, Richard, *The Rise of the Creative Class: And How It's Transforming Work, Leisure, Community, and Everyday Life*, Basic Books (New York), 2002

Gandy, Matthew, 'Cyborg Urbanization: Complexity and Monstrosity in the Contemporary City', *International Journal of Urban and Regional Research*, vol 29, no 1, March 2005, pp 26–49

Gershenfeld, Neil A, *Fab: The Coming Revolution on Your Desktop – From Personal Computers to Personal Fabrication*, Basic Books (New York), 2005

Glaeser, Edward, *Triumph of the City: How Our Greatest Invention Makes Us Richer, Smarter, Greener, Healthier, and Happier*, Penguin Press (New York), 2011

Goldstein, Brett and Dyson, Lauren, *Beyond Transparency: Open Data and the Future of Civic Innovation*, Code for America (San Francisco), 2013

Gordon, Eric and de Souza e Silva, Adriana, *Net Locality: Why Location Matters in a Networked World*, Wiley-Blackwell (Chichester), 2011

Graham, Stephen and Marvin, Simon, *Splintering Urbanism: Networked Infrastructures, Technological Mobilities and the Urban Condition*, Routledge (London and New York), 2001

Greenfield, Adam, *Against the Smart City: A Pamphlet*, Verso (New York), 2013

Jasanoff, Sheila (ed), *States of Knowledge: The Co-Production of Science and the Social Order*, Routledge (New York), 2004

Katz, James E and Rice, Ronald E, *Social Consequences of Internet Use:*

*Access, Involvement, and Interaction*, MIT Press (Cambridge, Massachusetts), 2002

Kurgan, Laura, *Close Up at a Distance: Mapping, Technology, and Politics*, Zone Books (New York), 2013

Medina, Eden, *Cybernetic Revolutionaries: Technology and Politics in Allende's Chile*, MIT Press (Cambridge, Massachusetts), 2011

Mitchell, William J, *City of Bits: Space, Place, and the Infobahn*, MIT Press (Cambridge, Massachusetts), 1995

Mitchell, William J, *Me++: The Cyborg Self and the Networked City*, MIT Press (Cambridge, Massachusetts), 2003

Nova, Nicolas, *Les Médias géolocalisés*: *Comprendre les nouveaux médias numériques*, FYP Éditions (Limoges), 2009

Nova, Nicolas, *Futurs? La Panne des imaginaires technologiques*, Les Moutons Électriques (Montélimar), 2014

November, Valérie, Camacho-Hübner, Eduardo and Latour, Bruno, 'Entering a Risky Territory: Space in the Age of Digital Navigation', *Environment and Planning D: Society and Space*, vol 28, no 4, 2010, pp 581–99

Offenhuber, Dietmar and Ratti, Carlo (eds), *Decoding the City: Urbanism in the Age of Big Data*, Birkhäuser (Basel), 2014

Picon, Antoine, *La Ville territoire des cyborgs*, Les Éditions de l'Imprimeur (Besançon), 1998

Picon, Antoine, *Digital Culture in Architecture: An Introduction for the Design Professions*, Birkhäuser (Basel), 2010

Picon, Antoine, *Ornament: The Politics of Architecture and Subjectivity*, Wiley (Chichester), 2013

Picon, Antoine, *La Ville des réseaux: Un imaginaire politique*, Éditions Manucius (Paris), 2014

Picon, Antoine and Robert, Jean-Paul, *Un Atlas parisien: Le dessus des cartes*, Éditions du Pavillon de l'Arsenal, Picard (Paris), 1999

Rancière, Jacques, *The Politics of Aesthetics* [*Le Partage du sensible: Esthétique et politique*, 2000], translated by Gabriel Rockhill, Continuum (London and New York), 2004

Rheingold, Howard, *Smart Mobs: The Next Social Revolution*, Perseus (Cambridge, Massachusetts), 2003

Sadler, Simon, *The Situationist City*, MIT Press (Cambridge, Massachusetts), 1998

Shepard, Mark (ed), *Sentient City: Ubiquitous Computing, Architecture, and the Future of Urban Space*, MIT Press (Cambridge, Massachusetts) and the Architectural League of New York (New York), 2011

Swyngedouw, Erik, 'Circulations and Metabolisms: (Hybrid) Natures and (Cyborg) Cities', *Science as Culture*, vol 15, no 2, June 2006, pp 105–21

Townsend, Anthony M, *Smart Cities: Big Data, Civic Hackers, and the Quest for a New Utopia*, WW Norton & Company (New York and London), 2013

Turkle, Sherry, *Life on the Screen: Identity in the Age of the Internet*, Simon & Schuster (New York), 1995

Virilio, Paul, *Ce qui arrive*, Actes Sud (Arles), 2002 (English version: *Unknown Quantity*, Thames & Hudson (London), 2003)

Wachter, Serge, *La Ville interactive: L'Architecture et l'urbanisme au risque du numérique et de l'écologie*, L'Harmattan (Paris), 2010

Zardini, Mirko (ed), *Sense of the City: An Alternative Approach to Urbanism*, Canadian Centre for Architecture (Montreal) and Lars Müller (Baden), 2005

Zreik, Khaldoun (ed), *Nouvelles cartographies, nouvelles villes: HyperUrbain.2*, Europia (Paris), 2010

# Index

Figures in *italics* type refer to captions

11 September attacks (2001) *54*

*2001: A Space Odyssey* (film) 13, 36, *37*, 78

## A

Accra, Ghana 140
  Agbogbloshie suburb *147*
Ahmedabad, India 23–4
Alexander, Christopher 77
algorithms 12, 29, 49, 82, 100, 106, 141
Allende, Salvador 73, *74*
Alphand, Jean-Charles *52*
Amazon 92, 135
ambient intelligence 32
Amsterdam, Netherlands: cargo plane crash (1992) *55*
animal rights 141
API (application programming interfaces) 125
Apple 33, 92
Arab Spring 84, *84*
'Arcology' 118
artificial intelligence 12, *12*, 71, 78, 141
  iCub robot *12*
Arts et Métiers ParisTech *108*
Ascher, François: 'tunnel effects' between distant highly developed districts *10*
atoms and data bits 61, 106, 107, 148
augmented reality 14, *15*, 17, 18, 24, 35, 105, 106, 107, *108*, 110, *111*, 113, 115, 138,

139, *139*

## B

B+H Architects *151*
Badham, John 58, *60*
Barcelona, Spain
  5D Smart City data visualization platform *127*
  22@Barcelona 112
  Museu d'Art Contemporani de Barcelona (Museum of Contemporary Art of Barcelona): 'You Are Here' exhibition (1995) 109, *109*
  Smart City Campus project *10*
barcodes 43
Bateson, Gregory 96
  *Steps to an Ecology of Mind* 80
Batty, Michael: *The New Science of Cities* 50
Beer, Stafford 73
Ben-Dov, Yoav *112*
Benedict XVI, Pope 77
Benjamin, Walter 99
Bentham, Jeremy 125, 153
Berkeley, Edmund Callis: *Giant Brains, or Machines that Can Think* 69
Berlin, Germany 109
Bin Laden, Osama 75
biometry 80, 91
Biostamp 80, *81*
*Blade Runner* (film) 70
Bordeaux, France 31

Borges, Jorge Luis: 'Del rigor en la ciencia' ('On Exactitude in Science') 134
Boston, Massachusetts 8, *18*, 149
  BanQ restaurant *47*
  Bridj buses 123, *124*
  'Citizens Connect' app 31, *32*
Branch, Melville Campbell 77
  city planning centre for Los Angeles 73, *73*
  conceptualised outcomes of continuous city planning *72*
Bridle, James 138
bulletin boards *33*, 43

## C

Cairo, Egypt: Tahrir Square 84, 85, *85*
Camacho-Hübner, Eduardo 135
Cambridge, Massachusetts: Kendall Square district 45, *48*
  *see also* Massachusetts Institute of Technology
Cameron, James 70
Canadian Centre for Architecture 44
Cap Digital 133
Cardon, Dominique 82
Carroll, Lewis: *Sylvie and Bruno Concluded* 134
Carticipe 130–31, *133*

# Picture Credits

The author and the publisher gratefully acknowledge the people who gave their permission to reproduce material in this book. While every effort has been made to contact copyright holders for their permission to reprint material, the publishers would be grateful to hear from any copyright holder who is not acknowledged here and will undertake to rectify any errors or omissions in future editions.

Cover image © Keiichi Matsuda

p 8 Image courtesy of IBM; p 10 © Urban Habitat – Barcelona City Council; p 11 © Michael Christopher Brown/Magnum Photos; p 12 © Emile Loreau/ISIR (UPMC/CNRS) lab/Picturetank; p 14 © Princeton University Library; published under the authority of the Electric Telegraph Company, by Day & Son, lithrs., Historic Maps Collection, Department of Rare Books and Special Collections, Princeton University Library; p 15 © HERE, a Nokia company; p 17 © Eric Fischer, using date from Flickr and Picasa. Base map © OpenStreetMap contributors, CC-BY-SA; p 18 © Ari Ofsevit. Base data from MassGIS, citation Office of Geographic Information (MassGIS), Commonwealth of Massachusetts, MassIT. Other data from the Metropolitan Area Planning Council and Hubway; p 19 © David Levene/The Guardian; p 20 © Alan McConchie; pp 25, 26 © 2015 Living PlanIT – All Rights Reserved; pp 28 & 29 Courtesy of Association des amis d'Albert Robida, - www.robida.info; p 30 © 2015, Foursquare Labs, Inc. All of the Foursquare ® logos and trademarks displayed in these screenshots are the property of Foursquare Labs, Inc.; p 32 © Connected Bits LLC; p 33 © www.siemens.com/press / Reprinted from Siemens' Pictures of the Future magazine; p 34 © Vox Media, www.TheVerge.com; p 35 © Umbrellium Limited; p 36 © 20th Century Fox / Everett Collection / Rex; p 37 Released in to the Public Domain, courtesy Wikipedia; p 38 © 2005 mailer_diablo. Creatove Cp,,pms Attributon-Share Alike 3.0 Unported License: http://creativecommons.org/licenses/by-sa/3.0/deed.en; p 39 © Google; p 40 © Senseable City Lab, MIT; p 41 © Photo by Philly Yi; p 42 (t) © Libelium Comunicaciones Distribuidas S.L.; p 42 (b) © Cyril Chigot; p 43 © CISCO France; p 45 © Antoine Picon; p 46 © Christian Richters; p 47 © John Horner; p 48 © Courtesy of MIT, © Elkus Manfredi Architects; p 49 © Image